Abbreviations Used in this Book

Tbs.	*tablespoon*
tsp.	*teaspoon*
oz.	*ounce*
lb.	*pound*

Equivalent Measures

1 teaspoon = 1/3 tablespoon
1 tablespoon = 3 teaspoons
2 tablespoons = 1 fluid ounce
2 tablespoons = 1/8 cup
4 tablespoons = 1/4 cup
5 tablespoons+1 teaspoon = 1/3 cup
8 tablespoons = 1/2 cup
1 cup = 8 fluid ounces
1 pint = 2 cups = 16 ounces
1 quart = 4 cups

Measuring Margarine and Butter

One stick = 8 Tbs. = 1/2 cup = 1/4 lb. = 4 oz.
Two sticks = 16 Tbs. = 1 cup = 1/2 lb. = 8 oz.
Four sticks = 32 Tbs. = 2 cups = 1 lb. = 16 oz.

1/2 oz	1 oz	1 1/2 oz	2 oz	2 1/2 oz	3 oz	3 1/2 oz	4 oz
1 Tbs.	2 Tbs.	3 Tbs.	4 Tbs.	5 Tbs.	6 Tbs.	7 Tbs.	8 Tbs.

The
BEGINNER'S
— KOSHER —
COOKBOOK

The BEGINNER'S — KOSHER — COOKBOOK

Seymour Fiedler

FELDHEIM PUBLISHERS
JERUSALEM • NEW YORK

Library of Congress Cataloging-in-Publication Data

Fiedler, Seymour.
    The beginner's kosher cookbook / by Seymour Fiedler.
       p. cm.
    Includes index.
    ISBN 0-87306-794-0.
    1. Cookery, Jewish.   I. Title.
TX724.F378 1997
641.5'67--dc21   97-8251

FELDHEIM PUBLISHERS
POB 35002 / Jerusalem, Israel

200 Airport Executive Park
Nanuet, NY 10954

Printed in Israel

Design and typesetting by Sarah Lipman

This book is dedicated
to the memory of two wonderful cooks:
my beloved wife and my beloved mother,
may they rest in peace.

My mother,

SARAH SIEGELWACHS FIEDLER ע״ה

was a devoted homemaker and the soul of goodness.

♦ *I will always remember when I was a small child, waking up
in the darkness of pre-dawn on Friday mornings,
to the indescribable aroma of my mother's freshly baked
challah, cinnamon rugelach, and potatonik.*

My wife,

OLGA MONDERER FIEDLER ע״ה

had a heart of gold.

♦ *I have been in the precious stone business most of my life,
but I have never had a diamond more precious.
I know what a jewel I had and I appreciated her
every day of our life together.*

ACKNOWLEDGMENTS

♦ ♦ ♦ ♦ ♦ ♦ ♦ ♦ ♦

I would like to express my gratitude and appreciation to some of my relatives and friends who gave me some very good recipes. We had no idea then that they would end up in *The Beginner's Kosher Cookbook*:

Annette Fiedler Mandis (my daughter)

Sylvia Nelson

Roberta Lerner

Gloria Grossman

Lilly Zohary

and to Malkah Cohen, who patiently typed the chapters of this book again and again, and who contributed a few of her own recipes as well.

I offer deepest thanks to Yaakov Feldheim and the staff of Feldheim Publishers in Jerusalem: Marsi Tabak, editor-in-chief, and the members of the editorial, production, and art departments for their professional work. Sarah Lipman's attractive design has greatly enhanced my book.

And to those whom I forgot to mention, I do appreciate all of your contributions, and I thank you all.

Seymour Fiedler
August 1997

TABLE OF CONTENTS

Introduction to Cooking

About Kosher Food

The Basics

Tips and Secrets

Seasoning the Food

Dear Reader,

There are many, many cookbooks available, full of recipes of every kind. But all these wonderful recipes won't help the person who has never cooked before and doesn't know where or how to begin. This cookbook is designed for the person who may have never even gone grocery shopping.

This book goes along with you to the supermarket, butcher shop, fish store, or fruit store, and tells you which foods to buy and which to avoid, which are healthy and which are not. Not only do I take you shopping, but after shopping, we will go home to your kitchen and put away the foods that we bought — into the freezer, the refrigerator, the kitchen cabinets, and some just in a glass bowl on the counter. After all that, we will start together to cook healthy, delicious, and nutritious kosher meals.

My cookbook does not overwhelm you with many hundreds of recipes. I give you a broad selection of different recipes to choose from for every meal. Most of the recipes are designed to get you out of the kitchen as fast as possible. There are a few that require longer preparation time, but I believe you will find that they are worthwhile when you enjoy the tasty results. You will end up with healthy and very delicious foods that will delight you — for breakfast, lunch, and supper.

This book is designed for the young man or woman who has just left the mother's nest, the young bride just learning to cook, and also for the widower who appreciates healthy, tasty food.

A widower faces a special problem. Not only must he cope with the loss of his lifelong companion, but now he has to assume responsibility for those tasks that were always his wife's concern. Of all, learning to cook can prove to be the most overwhelming. Sure, he may be able to go to his children for a meal or two, but after a few times, he will want to feel independent.

I was faced with such a situation in 1986 when I lost my dear wife after thirty-eight happy years of marriage. I coped with my problem for a few months. Then I noticed that my suits were a size or two too big on me. Life was at its lowest ebb, to say the least, and a solution had to be found.

You see, I was very spoiled when it came to food. My mother, may she rest in peace, was not a rocket scientist or a brain surgeon, but when it came to traditional kosher cooking, she could have gotten a Ph.D. A few of her recipes ended up with my sister and some with my wife, who kept an index file of her recipes. And my beloved wife, may she rest in peace, continued in my mother's tradition to provide me with delicious meals.

At first, after I became a widower, I tried to eat in restaurants, but I hated to wait thirty minutes for a three-minute egg! The kosher eateries are often far away and can be difficult to travel to. Also, it can be quite expensive to eat out all the time. And besides that, after hearing about what goes on in restaurant kitchens, I decided not to go out to eat too often.

Of course, there are always the takeout food stores. I tried them. Sometimes you do get a tasty chicken, if you are lucky enough to get a freshly cooked one. Unfortunately, quite often I got a chicken that was cooked two days earlier, even though I asked for a fresh chicken, cooked that day. It tasted stale and old and had no *ta'am* (flavor). The potato kugel was often dry and lacked the flavor and texture of my wife's kugel. Their soups are often fairly good, but I suspect they use monosodium glutamate and schmaltz (chicken fat) to enhance the taste in all their cooking. Monosodium glutamate is not tolerated by everyone, and nutritionists say schmaltz is pure cholesterol, which they blame for clogged arteries and heart attacks!

One time, I went with a friend to a restaurant. My friend said to me, "Try the Salisbury steak. It's really good here."

I told him, "I don't eat steak."

He laughed. "It's hamburger!"

"That's a pretty fancy name for hamburger."

"Well," he said, "There is another name for it."

"What is it?"

"Holy food."

"Why 'holy food'?" I asked, puzzled.

He smiled. "Because only God knows what's in it!"

Of course, that was only a joke, but the fact is, you really don't know what you're eating, or when it was cooked, unless you cook the food yourself.

So, I finally decided to cook a meal for myself. When I'd actually managed to make hamburgers, mashed potatoes, and green peas from a can, it was the most delicious meal I'd had in a long while. I knew then that I would not starve to death, and that I would not go to restaurants anymore.

After that, I started asking all my lady friends

how to cook this and that, and I kept adding to my wife's recipe file whenever I ate something that was tasty. Now I have quite a collection of recipes in that file, and I have chosen the best and the easiest ones to include in this book.

Some of my friends have asked me, "Why do you want to write a cookbook?" Here is one of my reasons: A few months ago, before I started on this project, a friend lost his wife. One morning, I went out early to buy a newspaper, and there was my friend, standing on the street corner!

I asked him, "What are you doing out here at 6:30 in the morning?"

"I'm waiting for the bakery to open so that I can get a buttered roll and a cup of coffee," he replied.

I realized that this was *me* a few years ago: afraid to try even the simplest task in the kitchen, on my own. I have come a long way since then.

There are some people who think they can't even learn to boil water. A lot of young people, and older ones, too, are afraid to cook because they have never cooked before. I want you to know that cooking is very rewarding and does not have to take up a lot of time. I have especially indicated throughout this book those dishes that take very little time to cook (and are tasty).

Although this book will teach you all the things you need to know, there's one thing you'll have to do by yourself — eat! But you should soon feel confident enough to invite a friend to join you for a meal.

ABOUT
KOSHER FOOD

Contributed by Rabbi Menachem Goldberger
in consultation with Rabbi Yitzchak Berkowitz.

The Jewish dietary laws — *kashrus* — can be divided into six different areas:

- kosher and non-kosher species;
- the preparation of permitted species and the removal of various non-kosher parts of the animal;
- the prohibition of mixing milk and meat;
- the Passover laws;
- food of non-Jews;
- laws regarding produce of the Land of Israel.

♦ A ♦
Kosher and non-kosher species

1 **Animals:** Only animals that chew their cud and have split hooves may be eaten, for example, cattle, sheep, goats, and deer.

2 **Fowl:** All fowl may be eaten — for example, chickens, geese, etc. — except for the forty or so non-kosher birds listed in the Torah. Practically speaking, since we are not certain as to the precise identity of the birds listed in the Torah, only birds for which there is an established tradition of *kashrus* may be eaten.

3 **Fish:** Only fish with fins and scales are kosher. See *Is it Kosher?* by Rabbi E. Eidlitz (Feldheim), for a complete list of kosher fish.

4 **Insects and worms:** No "swarming creature" — whether of land or water, or those that fly — may be eaten. Although the Torah does permit consumption of certain types of locust, their identities are no longer known in most Jewish communities. (Yemenite Jewry does have a tradition about permissible types of locust.) This set of prohibitions greatly affects the preparation of food. (See *Appendix B* for *very important* information on checking food for insects.)

♦ B ♦
The preparation of permitted species and the removal of various non-kosher parts

1 **Shechitah (ritual slaughter):** Meat from a kosher animal may not be eaten unless the animal was slaughtered according to Jewish law. If an animal or bird dies in any other way, it may not be eaten. Fish do not need *shechitah*.

Shechitah consists of a horizontal cut across the windpipe and gullet of the animal with a knife free of any nicks. The cut must be made without interruption by a to-and-fro movement (without downward pressure). Observance of these laws ensures a painless death for the animal.

2 **Treifah (non-kosher):** An animal that would be classified by halachic standards as diseased or injured before it was slaughtered, is not kosher. This is called *treifah* or *treif*. Halachah — Jewish law — does not call for the examination of every limb and organ of the slaughtered animal before consumption, as most diseases and injuries are uncommon, but if one notices abnormal discoloration in the internal organs of fowl, a rabbi should be consulted.

The most problematic organ in animals is the

lung. Halachah calls for careful inspection of an animal's lungs to ascertain that they have not been punctured in a way that would render the animal *treifah*. The meat of an animal whose lungs are found to be perfectly free of any lesions is labeled *chalak*, or *glatt*, in Yiddish, meaning "smooth." Meat does not have to be *glatt* to be certified as kosher. All meat should be bought only from a source certified as kosher by a reliable rabbinic authority.

3 **Chelev:** Certain fats (primarily the fatty membranes that envelop internal organs) of kosher animals may not be eaten and are removed after slaughtering. Birds and non-domesticated animals (such as deer) have no forbidden fat.

4 **Gid ha-Nasheh (the sciatic nerve):** The sciatic nerve of an animal (not a bird) may not be eaten. In order to render the meat of an animal kosher, its sciatic nerve, the *chelev*, and various arteries must be removed. This process is known as *nikkur* in Hebrew, *traibering* in Yiddish, and porging in English. The process of porging the hindquarters of an animal involves so much tedious skilled labor that slaughterhouses forgo use of the hindquarters altogether, and sell it unporged as non-kosher meat. Consequently, many popular cuts of meat are unavailable to the kosher consumer. In Israel, porging of the hindquarters is more common.

5 **Blood:** The blood of an animal or bird may not be eaten. Therefore, after slaughtering, the blood must be drained and the arteries porged.

Blood within the meat is removed by "kashering" — soaking and salting — or broiling (except for liver, for which only the broiling process is acceptable). (See *Appendix A*.)

Kashering meat, until relatively recently, used to be one of the most important skills necessary for keeping a kosher kitchen. Today, however, most kosher meat is sold already kashered.

A speck of blood found in a fertilized egg renders the egg non-kosher. Therefore, it is customary to break each egg separately into a glass, to check for blood spots. It is also customary, when boiling eggs, to boil at least three together so that if one contains a speck of blood the other two "outnumber" it and it is considered kosher. Today, however, commercial eggs are not fertilized, and thus a spot of blood does not render them non-kosher. Therefore only the blood spot, and not the entire egg, is discarded. Nevertheless, many people still retain the above customs.

♦ C ♦
The prohibition of mixing meat and milk

The Torah, in three different places, repeats the verse: "You shall not cook a kid in its mother's milk." The Rabbis of the Talmud interpreted this as a general prohibition against cooking, eating, or benefiting from, any meat cooked in milk.

By Rabbinic prohibition, meat and milk cannot be eaten together even if they have not been cooked together. Jewish law requires that one wait before eating milk or milk products after having eaten meat products, with custom varying from one to six hours (six being the most common custom). After eating milk or milk products one need not wait before eating meat, but should drink something or rinse his mouth thoroughly, and chew something — preferably parve bread, crackers, cookies, or cake — in order to remove the remainder of the milk product in his mouth, and then wash his hands before eating meat. Some

also wait half an hour. If one has eaten hard cheese aged for more than six months, the custom is to wait before having meat the same amount of time that one is accustomed to wait between meat and milk.

Milk and meat may not be eaten by two people at the same time at the same table, unless there is some separation between them, or they are eating on separate tablecloths or placemats. In order to observe all these laws carefully, we use separate cooking and eating utensils for milk and meat. Knives not used for milk or meat should be used for slicing bread and vegetables. Dairy and meat dishes should be washed separately, using different dishpans and sponges.

If milk and meat are mixed or if they come into contact with a utensil of the other type, a competent rabbi should be consulted. (This would also apply to non-kosher food which was mixed with kosher food.)

Parve foods — fish, grains and cereals, pulses, fruits, vegetables, spices, etc. — are neither dairy nor meat products and can be eaten with either.

(The Talmud considers the eating of meat and fish together as dangerous. Therefore, if one eats fish, he should drink or eat something — preferably parve bread, crackers, cookies, or cake — before eating meat. One should also clean the fish utensils he used, before using them for meat.)

♦ D ♦
Passover

The Torah forbids the consumption, benefit, and even possession of leavened foods — *chametz* — during the days of Passover. Matzos themselves need to be baked under strict supervision to ensure that the dough does not rise. (Matzah without proper supervision for Passover *may not* be eaten on Passover.)

Customarily, most Jewish homes have separate sets of cooking and eating utensils set aside for Passover. However, if one wants to use his regular cooking and eating utensils on Passover, they must be kashered in order to remove leaven which might be embedded in them. This should be done in consultation with a rabbi.

Leaven may not remain in a Jew's possession during Passover, but must be removed beforehand. One method used to rid oneself of leaven is to sell it to a non-Jew. Leaven which remained in Jewish possession during Passover may not be eaten after Passover.

◆ E ◆
Foods of non-Jews

Before the destruction of the Second Temple, the Rabbis decreed several prohibitions to minimize socializing between Jew and non-Jew, as a way to prevent assimilation. Additionally, they required the supervision of dairy products to ensure that all ingredients would be of kosher origin.

1 **Wine:** Wine which is handled by non-Jews may not be consumed by Jews. This applies also to grape juice, vinegar, or distilled wine such as brandy. Kosher wine which is handled by a non-Jew may be consumed if it is doubly sealed or sealed in a foolproof manner. Once boiled, kosher wine is unaffected by non-Jewish handling.

2 *Food cooked by non-Jews:* Food cooked by non-Jews may not be eaten if the food in question could not have been eaten raw and is the kind of food one would serve at a social event. Bread baked by a non-Jew, however, is permitted if it has proper *kashrus* supervision.

3 *Milk and cheese:* Milk from a non-kosher animal (whether a non-kosher species or a *treifah*) is not kosher. Jewish law therefore requires that a Jew supervise the milking to ensure that no milk from a non-kosher animal was added. Cheese, too, must have *kashrus* supervision to ensure that non-kosher rennet was not used in processing.

♦ F ♦
Laws regarding produce of the Land of Israel

These laws are quite complex and only the basics will be discussed here.

1 *Tithes:* The Torah teaches us that produce grown in the Land of Israel is holy and that one may not partake of it without prior separation of *terumos* and *ma'asros* — the tithes. In all, some twenty percent of all produce is to be separated, and, during the time of the Holy Temple in Jerusalem, distributed among *kohanim*, Levites, or the poor, or to be eaten in Jerusalem under conditions of ritual purity. (Nowadays, it is discarded.) When buying Israeli produce (whether in Israel or elsewhere), one must either insist on proper certification that tithes have been separated, or separate the tithes himself. For details of the tithing process, see *Eretz Ha-Tzvi*, by Rabbi Zvi Teichman (Feldheim).

2 *Orlah and Revai:* Fruit grown within the first three years of a tree's life may not be eaten.

While this prohibition applies both in the Land of Israel and outside it, halachically, one is not required to suspect that a fruit is *orlah* unless it was grown in Israel. Many fresh fruits and processed foods whose ingredients include fruit, come with certification stating they are free of *orlah*. Many authorities permit even Israeli fruit without certification, provided that the majority of that particular strain of fruit is known not to be *orlah*. Fruit of the fourth year is called *neta revai*, and must undergo a process of redemption. This is generally included in the tithing process (see above).

3 ***Chadash (new):*** The Torah does not permit partaking of new grain that took root from after Passover until the following Passover (more precisely, the first intermediate day of Passover). Outside Israel, the accepted practice is to assume that all grain and grain products are *yashan*, of an earlier harvest and permissible. In Israel, the Rabbinate sees to it that local *chadash* does not reach the consumer.

4 ***Challah:*** The Torah instructs us to separate a portion — called the *challah* — of all dough made from grain grown in the Land of Israel and to present it to a *kohen* who is to eat it in ritual purity. (Jewish law includes only five species in the category of grain: wheat, barley, spelt, oats, and rye.) The Rabbis extended this commandment to include dough made of grain grown outside the Land of Israel as well.

The requirement to separate *challah* applies only to a dough, or a series of doughs, made of a substantial quantity of flour. There is no need for *challah* to be taken from dough that contains less than 1200 grams, or 2 pounds, 11 ounces, of flour.

The separation involves removing some dough — a piece approximately the size of half an egg, reciting the blessing, and then declaring it to be *challah*. The blessing should not be said unless the dough contains at least 1666 grams, or 3 pounds, 11 ounces of flour; others insist on a minimum of 2250 grams, or about 5 pounds.

Nowadays, because ritual purity is unattainable, rather than presenting the *challah* to a *kohen,* it is burned or discarded.

For further information on the *mitzvah* of *challah,* see *Shmirath Shabbath K'hilchata* by Rabbi Y. Y. Neuwirth (Moriah, Jerusalem), chapter 42. (This is also available in English from Feldheim Publishers.)

5 **Shemittah — the Sabbatical year:** The Torah instructs that every seventh year the soil of the Land of Israel is to lie fallow. This is known as *shemittah.*

All produce that grew during the Shemittah year is considered holy, cannot be sold commercially, and is to be eaten in accordance with the laws of *shemittah.*

As a way of preventing the violation of *shemittah* laws, the Rabbis prohibited altogether the consumption of grain, legumes, and vegetables that grew during the *shemittah.* Authorities differ as to the status of fruit grown in violation of the laws of *shemittah,* as well as the status of non-Jewish produce grown in the Land of Israel.

Heter mechirah, a halachic device arranged by the Rabbinate involving the "sale" of the Land of Israel to non-Jews for the *shemittah* year is relied upon by many as a way of circumventing the *shemittah* laws; others do not accept this as valid.

Having discussed briefly the major issues in *kashrus*, we see how much effort is involved in ensuring that our food is kosher. Fortunately, there are *kashrus* organizations today that do most of the work for us and provide certification for all food products. For a listing of many reliable *kashrus* organizations, see *Is it Kosher? Encyclopedia of Kosher Food Facts and Fallacies* by Rabbi E. Eidlitz (Feldheim Publishers). (The customer should be aware that the letter "K" appearing on a food product cannot be taken as reliable proof of kosher supervision.)

For those interested in an in-depth presentation of the laws of *kashrus*, I highly recommend the two-volume *The Jewish Dietary Laws* by Dayan I. Grunfeld (Soncino Press), and *A Practical Guide to Kashruth* by Rabbi S. Wagschal (Feldheim Publishers).

THE BASICS

We often hear people who don't know how to cook
saying, "Me? Cook? I can't even boil water!"
And so let's start at the very beginning
and learn some basic skills that you will need
for almost all of your cooking.
Beginning with, what else?...

◆　◆　◆　◆　◆　◆　◆　◆　◆

How to Boil Water

1 Pour some cold water into a small pot or a whistling tea kettle. Heat over medium flame until the water bubbles vigorously in the pot, or the tea kettle whistles loudly, or until the steam comes out full force from the pouring spout of a non-whistling tea kettle.

2 Now you can make yourself a cup of coffee or tea. Pour the boiled water into a cup and either put in your instant coffee or dip in your teabag (see below).

Instant Coffee

All you have to do is boil some water, pour it into a cup, and spoon in as much instant coffee as you like. The normal amount is 1 tsp. per cup (more or less for stronger or weaker coffee, respectively). Or, you can put the coffee in the empty cup and pour the boiling water over it. Add milk and sugar as you like, and your coffee is ready.

Fresh Perked Coffee

Pour 3 or more cups of cold water into coffee pot. In the grinds section of your percolator, put one coffee measuring spoon of coffee for each cup of water, plus one more "for the pot." *Most people put a paper filter into the grinds section before the coffee is put in.* Bring to a boil, reduce flame to a simmer, and let it perk for 8 minutes. Let coffee cool off for 2 minutes and you have real coffee.

Tea

For a nice cup of tea, follow the directions above for boiling water. Then, pour it into a cup and add a teabag (or put the teabag in first). Leave the teabag in the boiled water for 1-2 minutes for mild flavor, 2-3 minutes for medium flavor, and 4-5 minutes for strong flavor. *I keep my teabag in the water for just half a minute — that seems strong enough for me.*

Iced Tea/Iced Coffee

Pour 1 cup of a little stronger tea into an 8 oz. glass. Add sugar, lemon or lemon juice, and mix, then fill the glass with ice cubes. Let stand for 5 minutes.

Use this same method for iced coffee, using instant coffee, but no lemon.

For larger amounts, prepare as many cups as you need. Then let it cool, pour it into a large container, and chill in refrigerator overnight.

TIPS AND SECRETS

Tips and secrets that only your mother would tell you!

♦　♦　♦　♦　♦　♦　♦　♦　♦

How to follow a recipe: You must read the *whole* recipe through before you begin so that you can see if you have all the ingredients. This will also tell you how much time you will need for preparation and cooking.

When you do begin cooking, it is a good idea (I do it all the time) to write down on a piece of paper what time you put the food into the oven or onto the stove to cook. Then mark down what time the food will need to be basted or turned, and when the food will be ready. This way, you won't have to rely only on your memory, especially when cooking two different foods at the same time.

Rubber gloves: Rubber gloves are very handy for many tasks besides washing dishes. I use them when peeling potatoes, carrots, and even onions! They have saved me a lot of scraped knuckles while grating potatoes and other vegetables on a hand grater. Gloves will also keep your skin from getting dry and chapped from a lot of washing. A kosher kitchen requires at least two pairs of gloves: one for meat and one for dairy. You might want a third for pareve foods like fish, fruits, and vegetables. You can tell them apart by marking them, or by using different colors for each purpose.

Torn gloves: If you are right-handed, you will wear out the right glove much faster than the left! After a while, you will find yourself with a nice collection of left-hand gloves that are still good. To make a new pair out of the old, turn one left glove inside out — making it a right-hand one — and mate it with another comparable left and you will have a "new" pair! If it's hard to pull the inverted glove onto your hand, sprinkle a little talcum powder into the glove and it will slip on without any trouble.

Pot-holders and oven mitts: Keep in mind that the oven, the stove, and your pots and pans are *going to get hot* when you cook. Anything which is that hot can burn you. Caution and prevention should be your guide words here. Many pots have handles that get hot and are hard to touch during cooking. For this purpose, it is good to have some small, thick pot-holders handy (separate ones for meat and dairy).

During baking and roasting, however, not only do you have to handle hot pans, but you often have to reach deep inside the oven. If you don't yet have quilted oven mitts, I highly recommend treating yourself to a pair of long ones, which cover part of your arm. They should prevent the risk of getting a bad burn on your arm from the sides of the oven or the racks.

Pots and pans: Always turn the handles of your pots inwards (toward the back of the stove) while cooking, so that your sleeve can't get caught on the handle and accidentally pull the pot off the stove. This is especially important when little children are around — they like to touch things that stick out at their eye level.

Frying pans: When tilting your frying pan to spread the oil or grease all over the pan, do it away from the stove and the flame, since a drop of grease into the flame can easily start a fire.

Candles: In Jewish homes, Shabbos candles are lit about 20 minutes before sunset on Friday evening, and *Yom Tov* candles before a Festival. Many fires have started with a little candle that fell off the candelabra. Be sure the candle is "cemented" into the cup by melting a bit of the bottom of the candle with a match, and then immediately pressing it into the cup of the holder. That will secure the candle. Also, always use a glass or metal tray under the candelabra, in case a candle should fall out. *Do not use any plastic around it*, as plastic burns very easily. And be sure to keep your candles well away from any curtains or shades that could be blown close to the flames by the wind from an open window.

It is also a good idea to keep a small fire extinguisher hanging on a wall in your kitchen. They are inexpensive, easy to use, and a useful tool in an emergency. I have had one for ten years (having it checked about every three years), and even though I have never had to use it, I just feel safer knowing that it's there.

First-aid hint: If you should get a burn on your hand, apply ice immediately or let cold water run over the burned spot for several minutes to help reduce the pain, to bring the skin's temperature down, and to prevent the burn from going deeper. DO NOT PUT GREASE OR BUTTER ON THE BURN! You will only increase the risk of infection! For any serious burn, see a doctor as soon as possible!

Thinking ahead: Keep a pad and pencil hanging from the refrigerator or a convenient wall in your kitchen for maintaining a list of all the items you are running low on. When your cereal box is ¾ finished, write it down, along with any other things you want to buy when you shop for the week. If you get into this good habit, you will never be out of what you need. (This is also a good place to jot down what time you started cooking a particular dish!)

Before going to bed, take out of the freezer what you want to cook the next day, and let it defrost. Also, if you plan to cook dried beans the next day, save yourself cooking time by soaking them overnight in a jar of water.

Boiling and simmering: Boiling is the rapid cooking of a liquid over a high flame. The liquid (usually water) will bubble vigorously and often develops a froth that can rapidly boil over the sides of the pot if not watched carefully. Simmering is slow cooking over a low flame, with the liquid coming more slowly to gentle bubbling (as with sauces and soups).

Frying: Frying is a skill you will need in preparing potato latkes, fish cakes, cauliflower cro-quettes, fried potatoes, and many other recipes. I always use a large 10" frying pan. Heat it for 2 or 3 minutes on a medium flame, and then pour in about 2 Tbs. of oil, any kind you like. Some people say that cooking sprays are healthier than oils, but I have found that when used in frying, they burn easily and can discol-or the food with some black grease. I use vegetable oil and sometimes olive oil. The important thing here is that you must always have enough oil in the frying pan, or your food will burn and spoil your meal. Therefore, when you see that the oil is low, pour another ½ to 1 Tbs. of oil into your frying pan. Tilt the pan so that the oil covers all areas. After frying food on one side, turn over and fry the other side. Always work with a fairly low flame (I call it

medium-low) — a large flame will burn up the oil faster and scorch the food.

How to peel vegetables: Hold the vegetable in your left hand, if you are right-handed (if you are left-handed do the reverse), and hold the vegetable at a 45° angle. Lean the tip of the vegetable on a cutting board or a plate and move the vegetable peeler from the middle of the vegetable toward the tip, turning the vegetable after each stroke. When one end is done, turn the vegetable upside down and do the other half the same way. Cut off the ends. Another way to peel vegetables is described in the *Vegetables: Handling and Preparation* chapter.

How to sauté vegetables: Cut up the food that you want to sauté: onions, celery, mushrooms, bell peppers, tomatoes, etc. Chop them or slice them — whatever the instructions call for. For example, they can be *diced* — cut into ¼" cubes, or *julienne-cut* — cut into matchlike strips.

Take a 10" skillet and heat it over a medium flame. Move the pan off the flame for a moment and carefully pour in 2-3 Tbs. of oil or spray it with oil spray about 3 times. Reduce your flame to low, return the pan to it, and pour in your vegetables. Keep mixing them with a spatula or fork until they reach the desired state. It is important to add a little more oil when the frying pan gets drier, or your vegetables will burn and have a bitter taste.

Steaming vegetables: When cooking vegetables, you have two main choices: You can boil them in a pot with just enough water to cover them, for 15-18 minutes (for most vegetables), or you can steam them, which nutritionists tell us is much healthier, because it retains more of the vitamins. A steamer is a large pot, with a perforated insert and a cover. Pour about 3-4 cups of water into the pot, bring it to a boil, and insert the rack. Place the vegetables into it and simmer for 4-10 minutes. The perforated insert allows the steam from the boiling water to cook the vegetables. You can put in a few different vegetables and steam them together. When the vegetables are done, remove the insert and serve. Do not leave the insert in the hot water, or the vegetables will get overcooked and soggy.

Basting food: When you bake a chicken or make a roast in the oven, the meat needs to be basted or it will dry out. There are two ways you can do this. You can use a large serving spoon, dip it into the sauce of whatever you are cooking, and spoon some of the sauce on top of the meat or fowl. Or, you can buy yourself a baster. This a useful and inexpensive gadget. Look for a picture of one in *Kitchen Tools* in *Appendix C*. A baster is a plastic tube about 7" long with a point that has a hole in it. On the other end, there is a rubber ball. You dip the pointed front into the sauce and squeeze the ball, letting out the air. When you release the ball, the tube fills with sauce. Hold the point over whatever you want to baste, then just press the ball again and the juice comes out.

To wash a baster, take a glass of hot soapy water. Squeeze and release the rubber ball to run the water into and out of the baster a few times. Repeat the process with a glass of hot clean water, let the water out, and then leave it to air dry.

Adding water: When adding water to your roast or other meats, do not pour the water on top of

the meat. That will rinse the seasoning off. Add the water to the sides of the pot or pan.

Broiling tips: When broiling anything in your oven's broiler, be sure to adjust the rack so that the food is 4-5" from the heat. This is especially true when using butter or margarine on the food. It could catch fire if it's too close to the flame! Set your temperature gauge to 475°-500°F. This should make your broiler sufficiently hot to broil your meat or fish (especially hamburgers, other patties, and fish fillets).

Broiling too long will dry out your meat and make the food leathery. Keep checking, because broiling even 2 minutes too long can ruin your meal!

Don't burn the food: When you cook a side dish that takes only 25 or 30 minutes, do not walk away from the kitchen and get involved in another project. Chances are you'll forget what's on the stove, and you'll burn your vegetables, pasta, or whatever you're cooking. Stay in the kitchen until the dish is done — check the seasoning, add more water when needed, stir the food, etc.

A kitchen timer is a valuable gadget to have for this purpose as well. Get one with a good, loud bell and perhaps you will be able to venture out of the kitchen while cooking after all!

Cutting bagels, rolls, etc.: Always cut with the sharp cutting edge of the knife *away* from yourself.

Keeping food warm: This is always a problem, since food gets cold very quickly after cooking or baking. Place the cooked food *covered* in a warm oven at the lowest setting, or turn off a hot oven, let it cool for 10 minutes, and place the covered food into the still-warm oven.

Time-savers: When slicing carrots, celery stalks, zucchini, etc., place two or three next to each other, hold your left hand over them gently to keep them in place, and slice them at the same time.

Baking pans: Quite often, a baking or frying pan may get a hard crust baked into the pan which is almost impossible to remove by normal washing, even with scouring powder. Just pour a little dishwashing detergent into the pan with some hot water and let it stand overnight. In the morning, it should come out easily with a metal scouring pad.

Caution: Do *not* use a metal scouring pad or scouring powder on any nonstick pan, as this will remove the nonstick film. Use only a soft plastic pad with some liquid soap.

Washing dishes: Always use hot water to wash your dishes, and use a good detergent — it will keep your dishes germ-free. Wear rubber gloves (see above) to avoid burning your hands, and to protect your skin from drying out.

After you have washed glassware, it may dry with visible water spots if left to dry on a drying rack. If you wipe them with your dish towel instead, they will be sparkling clean.

Cleaning the kitchen: While peeling potatoes, onions, carrots, or anything else, sponge the peels into your garbage can as soon as you finish peeling. If you drop peels on the kitchen floor, pick them up promptly. They are very

slippery — if you step on them, you could slip and hurt yourself.

Always clean off your counters as you cook. Also, wash all used mixing bowls and other dishes while the food is cooking — or your kitchen will look as if a hurricane has hit it!

You will touch the handles of your kitchen cabinets often while cooking, and your hands may be greasy from the food your are working with. After you finish cooking, wipe the handles with a damp sponge, so that you don't let the grease build up, making it harder to remove later.

Separating eggs: To separate the white of the egg from the yolk, crack the egg and carefully allow the liquidy white to run off into a glass or small bowl, while keeping the yolk in the egg shell. You can also use an egg separator. Remember to check for blood spots — see pg. 19.

Beating egg whites: Beating egg whites is easiest using an electric hand mixer. Beat the egg white at high speed for about 3-5 minutes until the white has turned into a snowy white thick consistency about 4 times its original size, and stiff peaks have formed. Making a "snow" from egg whites is usually needed when making soufflés, some cakes, and pies with meringue topping.

Salmonella: Eggs and uncooked chickens must not be left unrefrigerated for prolonged periods. Bacteria can grow and could lead to serious spoilage and salmonella poisoning. It is best to freeze raw chickens that you don't intend to cook immediately. Eggs are most safely stored in the refrigerator. Work surfaces, cutting boards, pots, pans, and utensils used in cooking and preparing food should be kept clean to prevent growth of bacteria.

A word about microwaves: Microwave cooking has become very popular in the last few years, due partly to the increasing affordability of microwave ovens. They can be very useful for people who find that they often have to prepare or warm food in a hurry. They are helpful for defrosting foods, heating up leftovers, baking a potato quickly, and warming liquids. Parts of many of the recipes in my book can be done in a microwave.

In spite of the popularity of microwaves, however, I still feel that you will get tastier results from cooking in a conventional oven. Foods that should be crisp, for example, will not come out that way in a microwave, which tends to leave foods soggy and rubbery. I do prefer conventional cooking and therefore, although you can adjust many of these recipes to microwave cooking, I do not give such instructions in my book.

SEASONING
THE FOOD

*A lot of the taste of food depends on
the quality and freshness of the ingredients used.
After that, the most important part of cooking
is the seasoning.
With the right seasoning, for example, even a
cheaper cut of meat can taste as good as a first cut.*

♦   ♦   ♦   ♦   ♦   ♦   ♦   ♦   ♦

While you are cooking, it is important for you to know which spices to add to the food you are preparing. And the best way to give the food the right taste is for you to taste it while it's cooking. Many cooks have a problem with this. What I do is, I put a spoon into the food, and then I lick the spoon. That way I know if I need to adjust the seasoning or not.

However, the final seasoning should be left for the end, when the food is almost ready, because very often, especially with liquids and semi-liquids like soup or gravy, the food gets condensed during cooking and what tasted just right in the beginning is too salty or too mild now. Therefore, leave a little room for the final adjustment.

Herbs

There are many people, especially after middle age, who are on restricted diets which prohibit such things as salt, sugar, etc. If you are one of these, you may have to make some adjustments, according to your doctor's instructions. However, in many cases there are simple substitutes you may be allowed to use instead of the ingredients specified.

For people who are on a restricted diet of no salt, certain herbs are a very good alternative. They give the food a good flavor and prove that you can eat tasty food without salt. In my *Chicken Recipes*, for example, I have a recipe seasoned only with herbs and spices, and it tastes delicious. It's called *Chicken with Oregano*. It's so good, that now I use it myself as my most frequent choice, and I don't even miss the salt. Neither will you. The *Chicken with Oregano* has an "exotic" taste. You will be very pleasantly surprised how good chicken and even vegetables can taste *without* salt.

Herbs and spices used to be very expensive until recently, when some enterprising companies started selling all kinds of exotic spices for down-to-earth prices. Most of them have the ⓤ symbol; therefore they are kosher, and parve.

Among the spices I like to use are: paprika, oregano, garlic powder, black pepper, and lemon peel. These spices can be used on fish, meats, and vegetables. Since some of these herbs are very sharp, a very small amount is needed.

It's difficult to mix small amounts of each in proper proportions. However, if you mix a substantial amount of each, according to the instructions, you'll have enough to last for a while. It would be advisable to save empty spice containers for this use, and of course, you must label each mixture, so that you will know what it is and what to use it with.

Then there is the simple garlic powder and pepper mixture I use instead of salt: four (4) teaspoons of garlic powder plus one-half teaspoon of black pepper. Shake it well to mix, then taste it to see if this proportion agrees with your taste. Increase or decrease ingredients accordingly.

Sprinkle one or more teaspoons of the mixture all over the chicken and bake according to instructions.

Among the other seasonings I use are: salt (or substitute), garlic (both fresh and powder), onions, lemon, honey, sugar, cinnamon, nutmeg, and soy sauce. Quite often, I will also put a bay leaf into fish sauce or soup and discard it after cooking. Then, there are also some vegetables that are used in cooking to enhance the taste, such as celery, carrots, tomatoes, and soup greens.

One very popular seasoning ingredient (which used to be one of my favorites) is instant soup powder or bouillon cubes. However, since there is some question about the advisability of eating monosodium glutamate (MSG), I have reduced my use of these products to a minimum. I always look at the ingredients on any package to see if there is any MSG in it. I use some such products, but only very, very rarely. There are some packaged foods that specify on the label "No MSG." I prefer to use these whenever possible.

Salt, pepper, and garlic

There is a big problem in describing the proportions of salt, pepper, and garlic powder to use in cooking. A larger piece of chicken or meat needs more than a smaller one. I use a salt shaker and just lightly dust the meat or chicken with salt. I then shake on very little pepper. I sprinkle on a little more garlic powder than I did the salt, because it's usually quite mild. Fresh garlic is much stronger. If I use any, I mince the garlic in a garlic press and then remove the garlic with my finger and rub it into the inside of the chicken (if I'm using a whole chicken). Then I spread the pulp on top of the chicken, along with the garlic powder. I do the same thing with roasts.

For the new cook, it may be better to use less pepper and salt and adjust the seasoning after the chicken or meat has been cooking for about 45 minutes to an hour. It will not harm you to lick the spoon, to get the taste (just wash the spoon afterwards)! You will quickly come to know more or less how much salt, pepper, and garlic powder you need to use to satisfy your own taste.

The salt issue

I had some friends over a while ago for dinner. One said, "You put too much salt into your cooking." The other friend took the salt shaker and added more salt. As you can see, everybody has his own taste. The first friend is on a "no salt" diet and is used to food without any salt; therefore every little bit of salt in the food is "too salty" for him.

What I've been doing lately is cooking the food without salt. Then I take off a portion for the guest on the no-salt diet and put that in a separate, small pot. After that, I add what I feel to be the proper amount of salt to the rest of the food, but the best way is to put salt and pepper shakers on the table and let your guests adjust the seasoning to their own taste.

Wine (and other liquids) in cooking

If you like the aroma of wine in your roast chickens or other roasted meat, you can add one-quarter to one-half of a cup of dry white wine (kosher, of course) to the pot. It gives the meat a nice aroma, but it's not for everyone. Try it once and see if you like it.

Sometimes I pour half a cup of orange juice

over the chicken instead of water, when I bake or roast a chicken. Some have even said this reduces the fat. I don't know if it does, but it gives the chicken a slightly different taste that you may enjoy.

What to do if...

If the food you cooked turned out to be too salty or spicy when you've finished cooking it, there are a few things you can still do to help correct it. (However, I must warn you, they don't always work.)

If the soup or gravy is too salty, you can either add more water and boil it a little longer, or you can put a peeled raw potato into the food while it's still cooking. The potato acts like a sponge and absorbs some of the salt. Discard the potato after the food is cooked, if it's too salty.

I was once invited to stay at a friend's house in Florida, and I decided to cook us a light meal for supper. I made *Salmon Croquettes* (see page 194). In Florida, they have something called Miami Spice. It has garlic powder and pepper in it, but no salt. It is quite mild, and you have to pour quite a lot of the powder into the food to really get the flavor. It is designed for older people and anyone else on a salt-free diet.

I made my mixture of salmon and all the other ingredients, and then kept pouring in what I thought was Miami Spice. It turned out to be pure pepper! It seems the same company also makes other spices, including pepper, and the labels look very similar. I kept shaking the powder into my mixture — at least two teaspoons of it — before I tasted it. When I did taste it, my mouth was on fire! My salmon croquettes seemed ruined, impossible to eat. Then I had an idea. Before throwing out all that money spent on a large can of red salmon, etc., I wanted to try to save it.

I put the whole mixture into a strainer, held it over the sink, and kept pouring cold water on the mixture, then squeezing the mixture to get the moisture out. It worked! All the pepper — and the other spices, too — were washed out. I then re-spiced the mixture and formed it into croquettes, fried them, and served them, as planned. I had saved the day and the salmon croquettes. My hosts loved them — they even took seconds!

The other day, I was preparing to roast a chick-en. While I was seasoning the chicken, I was also listening to a radio talk show. I did not realize that I had sprinkled too much salt, until an hour later when I tasted the chicken — it was much too salty! I poured off the gravy and kept it, which was okay, because I would be adding water to it later, any-way. I boiled some water in my kettle and poured some over the chicken. I shook the pot a little and poured it out. I then turned the chicken over and did the same thing on that side. Then I poured a little more boiled water over the chicken and put it back into the oven for three minutes. I then tasted a little piece and, to my surprise, the chicken tast-ed just right.

Sometimes you have to use your imagination and ingenuity to save a dish.

Let's Go Shopping

HOW TO BUY
FRUITS AND
VEGETABLES

*Nutritionists tell us we need at least
five fruit or vegetable servings in our diet each day.*

♦   ♦   ♦   ♦   ♦   ♦   ♦   ♦   ♦

There are many different kinds of fruits and vegetables available. In this section, we will look at a number of the most common ones and learn how to choose them for quality and freshness. We will also find out about how long each of them will last, and how to store them. Most fruits and vegetables must be refrigerated after they are ripe, or they will soon spoil. Some do better on a kitchen counter until they are ripe enough to eat or to store in the refrigerator.

Fruits

There are all kinds of fruits on the market. Many of them are in season only at specific times of the year, yet you can buy some of the summer fruits even in the middle of winter. They come from the southern states or California, or from South America and other countries. However, I find that foreign crops are often dry and not as sweet and tasty as our own American produce — and, of course, they are more expensive. We will deal here mostly with domestic fruits.

A hint: Bananas, apples, and pears discolor very quickly after you peel and slice them. Therefore, when using them as baking ingredients or in fruit salads, it is recommended that you mix them in a bowl with some lemon or orange juice, cover the dish with plastic wrap, and refrigerate them. This will help keep them from discoloring for a while.

Dried fruits such as apple, pear, plum, apricot, banana, and papaya last a long time and are usually served as a "nosh." They can also be cooked with carrots (see *Tzimmes*, pg. 109).

Frozen and canned vegetables

Many times, especially during the winter months or when certain vegetables are out of season, I buy frozen vegetables. They take only a few minutes to cook, since they are already steamed before they are frozen. They can be mixed with fresh vegetables and taste just fine. They save a lot of work and are handy when you are in a hurry.

I also like the very best canned sweet peas. They are very tasty and usually don't need any seasoning. You may want to keep in mind that, unless the can says, "no salt added," "low sodium," or "salt-free," canned vegetables are usually very high in salt.

When buying canned or frozen fruits and vegetables, remember to check for *kashrus* certification. Fresh fruits and vegetables should be checked carefully for insects and worms (see pg. 288). Especially problematic are green, leafy vegetables like cabbage, lettuce, and spinach, as well as scallions and corn on the cob. There are insect-free vegetables grown in special certified greenhouses that do not require checking.

	How to Choose	How to Store	How to Serve
Apples	There are many varieties of apples. The most popular sweet kinds are: Golden Delicious, Red Delicious, McIntosh, Cortland and Rome. Granny Smith are tart. The last three are mostly for cooking and baking. The first three are for eating. Look for even color; avoid bruised apples.	Refrigerate. Will last 2-3 weeks.	Raw, peeled or unpeeled, cooked, or baked.
Apricots	Best when they are firm and have a reddish glow. Avoid bruised apricots; they will spoil sooner.	Leave outside refrigerator to soften for 1-3 days, then refrigerate.	Raw, or baked in cakes or pies, or cooked in fruit soups.
Bananas	Buy bananas when they are firm and golden in color, but with some green still by the stem. They ripen very fast and discolor after a few days. The more green they are when you buy them, the longer they will last. Buy only what you will need, because of spoilage.	Bananas will turn brown in the refrigerator, but will stay white inside a few days longer than on the counter. Some people enjoy them frozen, too.	Raw.
Blueberries	These are usually easy to buy. Look for even, blue color; check for firmness.	Refrigerate.	Raw, with sour cream, baked in cakes and pies.
Cantaloupe	These are often too soft or too hard. Stem area softens and allows the scent of the fruit through as it ripens. It seems to be pot luck, but the good ones are very delicious. The same instructions go for *Honeydew melons*. Avoid those with soft spots as they were probably damaged in transit.	Hard ones have to be put on the counter at room temperature, sometimes for as much as a week. Some may be dry and not sweet enough (a little sugar may help). Refrigerate when ripe.	In wedges, diced, or balled into salads.

	How to Choose	How to Store	How to Serve
Cherries	These come out in early June, often disappearing by mid-July, and are high in calories. The best are Bing cherries. The best are dark red, large, and firm. Avoid soft, over-ripe, and spoiled cherries.	Cherries last only a few days, even in the refrigerator, before they spoil.	Raw, baked, or cooked.
Grapefruit	I use two types. Pink grapefruit is sweeter and, to me, tastes better than the white which is sour and needs sugar when eating them. The ones with smooth skin that are heavy for their size have more juice.	Refrigerate.	Cut in half, run a knife down the section membranes to make the sections easier to remove. Sprinkle some sugar on the cut-open surface (optional). Can also be peeled and eaten.
Grapes	I like both the green and red seedless varieties. They are ideal to eat as they are and also in fruit salads. Check for brown or soft grapes at the bottom of the box.	Refrigerate.	Raw and in salads.
Honeydew Melon	See *Cantaloupe.*	Refrigerate after it's ripe.	In wedges, diced, or balled in salads.
Kiwi	These are small with a brown, fuzzy outside. Inside, they have a pretty green color. They are juicy and have a very nice design. They should be firm; very soft ones are over-ripe.	Refrigerate.	Kiwis can be eaten peeled or sliced, with the outer skin removed. They make a very decorative effect on a vegetable or fruit platter.
Lemons	Pick firm ones with an even, yellow-gold color. They are used to both sweeten *and* sour, and are frequently used to garnish salads, fish, and other dishes.	Refrigerate.	Slice into tea or mixed drinks or as garnish, or squeeze for juice.

How to Choose Fruit

	How to Choose	How to Store	How to Serve
Mangoes	This is a very sweet fruit, if you can get to the meat. It is rather hard to peel. (See *How to Serve It.*) It usually becomes messy, but it has a very sweet and delicious taste. The yellow ones with a red glow are sweeter.	On counter until soft, then refrigerate.	Raw. The best way is to cut the skin, lengthwise, all around, into four sections, then peel the skin back. You can then cut the meat into long strips down to the large pit. Good in fruit salads.
Nectarines	See *Peaches*.	On counter until soft, then refrigerate.	Raw.
Oranges	These are very healthy and easy to buy. Just look for the firm, eating type. The pale ones with thin skin are used mostly for juice. Pick the deep orange color with thick skin; they are usually sweeter.	Refrigerate.	Raw, as a fruit in salads, or drink the juice.
Peaches	Peaches are available from May until September. Buy firm ones, leaving them on the counter to ripen in 2-3 days. Those with red colors are sweeter. Avoid those with brown spots. The same rules apply to *Nectarines*. The best peaches are Freestone.	On counter until soft, then refrigerate.	Raw, or in salads, or cooked in fruit soup. Also, baked in cakes or pies.
Pears	The most popular pears are Bartlett, Comice, Bosc, and Anjou. Bosc are brown in color and are dry. All others are green. Some have a reddish glow and are usually sweeter. The Comice are very juicy and sweet. Anjou and Bartlett are also good, but not as juicy and sweet. Buy them when they are firm, and avoid the ones with brown blemishes.	Leave them on the counter for a few days, if not yet ripe. After ripening, refrigerate.	Raw, peeled or unpeeled, in salads, or cooked as a dessert.

	How to Choose	**How to Store**	**How to Serve**
Pineapples	Pick light brown ones. They take 5 or more days to ripen. When ripe they have a pleasant odor, are soft on top, and the leaves come out easily.	On counter until ripe; then refrigerate.	Cut into slices; then remove peel and cut into chunks. Mixes well with cantaloupe and honeydew melon.
Plums	Large, dark blue plums get soft after a few days and are juicy. Red plums are not as sweet. The large green-gold colored plum is a bit tart. The small oval Italian plums are sweet and tasty, but spoil quickly. Dried prunes are made from these. Pick firm plums with deep, clear colors.	On counter until soft; then refrigerate.	Raw, or cooked in pies, cakes.
Strawberries	Buy these loose, if you can pick them, but they usually come packed in a little pint basket. Look for even red color, especially at the bottom of the basket, where some grocers try to hide green berries.	Refrigerate; use within 2-3 days.	Trim off the green stems and any overripe areas. See recipes.
Tangerines	These come out in the fall. They have a soft skin and peel easily. Some are very sweet. Pick the larger sizes, with deep orange colors. Small ones are good, too.	Refrigerate.	Raw as a fruit, or in fruit salads.
Watermelon	They are usually ready to eat when you buy them. The sweet ones are deep red with dark pits. Today there are some watermelons that have no pits and are easier to eat. There are also specialty melons with a golden pulp that is said to be high in beta carotene.	Refrigerate.	As a fruit or in salads, cut into balls or chunks.

	How to Choose	How to Store	How to Use
Asparagus	These are available in early summer, when they are quite reasonably priced. At other times, they can cost as much as $5 a pound. The young ones are thin and tasty. When they get bigger, they have white ends that are woody and which do not get soft when boiled.	Refrigerate. Will last only a few days.	Cooked. Cut off the white ends before boiling.
Avocado	Buy the ones with tight grain on the peel. Avoid the very soft ones— they are overripe and will not last. Most are very hard.	Keep hard avocados outside the refrigerator for 3-5 days, until they give a little to the touch, then put them into the refrigerator. Cut them into quarters and remove the skin. Wrap leftovers in foil and twist ends. Leave the pit in. Avocados will only last a few days. When the meat gets dark, remove it by scraping with a spoon or knife.	Raw.
Beets	Beets are sold in bunches. They are brown-skinned, with red meat and some leaves on top. Buy firm ones.	Refrigerate.	Cooked.
Broccoli	Get the dark green color; the ones turning yellow on top are getting old. Best when florets are tight.	Refrigerate. Will only last 4-5 days.	Raw, cooked, or steamed.
Brussels Sprouts	These look like small heads of cabbage. Buy the softer ones; the hard ones are older.	Refrigerate.	Cooked.

	How to Choose	How to Store	How to Use
Carrots	Look for deep orange, smooth color. There are a few different ways to buy them. They can come in cellophane bags, or you can buy them in a bunch, which are often just a bit fresher. Carrots also come in miniature, "baby" size, which are especially good raw.	Refrigerate. They will stay firm and last two weeks or more wrapped in a paper towel, then in a plastic bag.	Raw or cooked.
Cauliflower	The better quality comes wrapped in plastic. Should be very white. Tan color means it's getting old, but it's still okay to buy for same-day use. Avoid black-spotted cauliflower. Pick tight florets.	Will last about one week in the refrigerator.	Raw or cooked.
Celery	Buy the medium-green color. The very dark green have a bitter taste. They will get lighter during storage.	Refrigerate. The ones in the plastic bag will last about two weeks in the refrigerator; if kept in the bag, wrapped in a paper towel, they will stay crispy. Use up the pale ones first. Wipe the inside of the bag and remaining pieces each time you take some out, or every few days.	Raw or cooked.
Corn	Sold on the cob. Pull the green husk leaves apart. Kernels should be plump and firm. I usually squeeze one kernel and taste it to see if the corn is sweet. I like those with mixed white and yellow kernels, usually very tasty and sweet.	Refrigeration not needed if using within two days, but will last longer in the refrigerator.	Cooked.

	How to Choose	How to Store	How to Use
Cucumbers	The small, thin, dark green cucumbers are tastier than the large thick ones, which can be watery. The very large cucumbers will last longer, but they are not as tasty. Get very firm ones — soft cucumbers will only last a few days, as do small cucumbers. Therefore, only buy supplies for a few days.	Store loosely in refrigerator. Do *not* leave in plastic bag. May last 3-4 days.	Raw.
Eggplant	There are various kinds. The baby eggplant is the same as the large one but costs more. They should be firm, not soft, with a deep, dark purple color.	Refrigerate. Will last up to one week.	Cooked.
Garlic	Fresh garlic is firm and juicy. Older garlic feels very soft and is dried out.	Refrigerate. Discard when very soft.	Raw or cooked.
Lettuce	There are many varieties of lettuce. We will only look at the "Iceberg" and "Romaine" varieties. Look for a dark green color, said to have the most vitamins. These also last longer in the refrigerator. Buy tight heads. Avoid wilted leaves or brown-spotted heads.	Keep all lettuce in refrigerator, tightly wrapped in a paper towel, then in plastic, preferably in the bag it came in. Wipe inside of plastic bag every few days or whenever you open it to take some leaves out.	Raw.
Okra	This is a thin, 2-3" long vegetable that can be used in vegetable soups or as a side dish. Pick the firm ones.	Refrigerate.	Cooked.

	How to Choose	How to Store	How to Use
Onions	There are many varieties, ranging from tiny "pearl" onions to large "Bermudas." I use the most common yellow onions, which often come in 2-3 lb. net bags. In early summer, there is the "Vidalia," which is mild and sweet, like "Spanish" onions. These are often used for salads. Buy firm onions.	Onions need air or they will spoil. Do not refrigerate. Store in bottom kitchen cabinet. Will last 2-3 weeks.	Raw, cooked, or sautéed.
Peppers, Red and Green (Bell)	These come also in other colors, such as yellow. "Sweet" or "Bell" varieties are mild. Buy firm, deep colors. Avoid soft, spotted peppers.	Refrigerate.	Raw, cooked, or sautéed.
Potatoes	There are quite a few varieties. I prefer the "Idaho," in 5-pound bags, but I also use white or red loose potatoes. In the spring, there are also small, "new" potatoes. Russet stay firmer after they are cooked.	Do not refrigerate. Store in lower kitchen cabinet. Original plastic bag usually has holes for ventilation.	Cooked.
Radishes	Buy the bunches rather then cello-bags. They are fresher and more tasty, although more expensive. The cello-bagged radishes are OK too, but watch for splits. Buy the smooth ones. The large black radishes are very sharp. The large white radishes are milder.	Refrigerate.	Raw.
Scallions (Green Onions)	These are long slender stalks, green with white, narrow bulbs, sold in bunches of five or six. Avoid ones with dried green leaves; they will not last long.	These will last a week to ten days in the vegetable bin of the refrigerator.	Raw or cooked.

	How to Choose	**How to Store**	**How to Use**
Spinach	A leafy vegetable. Choose for dark green color and crispness.	This vegetable is very sandy and must be washed a few times to remove all the sand. Remove stems before serving in salad or boiling.	Raw or cooked.
String Beans (Green Beans)	String beans come in several varieties. The most popular and tastiest are the light or dark green string beans. Pick firm ones. Spotted ones are getting old. Avoid soft ones, unless you will cook them the same day.	Refrigerate in a paper bag.	Raw or cooked.
Sweet Potatoes & Yams	These are quite large and are often baked in the oven with roasting chicken or other meat. Yams are pink in color and are drier. Sweet potatoes, which I prefer, are orangy-brown in color, more moist, and a little sweeter.	Best if refrigerated in vegetable bin.	Cooked or baked.
Tomatoes	Pick the very red color. Should be firm. Buy a few that are still partially green and leave them out in a dish on the counter to ripen. You may also want one or two softer ones for use that same day or the next day.	Leave unripe ones on the counter to ripen. Ripe ones will last about 4-7 days in the refrigerator.	Raw or cooked.
Zucchini	Dark green and firm. Do not buy soft ones.	Refrigerate. Will last only 4-5 days.	Raw, cooked, or fried.

HOW TO BUY
POULTRY
AND MEAT

♦　♦　♦　♦　♦　♦　♦　♦　♦

I do most of my shopping on Thursday for the weekend and the rest of the week. I find the best time to shop is around noon, because then mothers of small children have to be home to feed their offspring, and the checkout counters are not too crowded.

Your meat market should have impeccable *kashrus* certification. I like to buy at a meat market that has a very large turnover, because the fresher the chicken or meat, the tastier the cooked meal will be. Since I don't like to run to the butcher every time I want to cook something, I buy extra meat, chicken, and fish products to put into the freezer. Frozen fowl, meats, and fish will last a long time in the freezer (up to six months), but they have to be solidly frozen, and they do lose a little of their taste in the freezing.

Most of my main dishes are made from fowl, veal, or fish. I very seldom buy beef, but I do buy veal. On very special occasions, I may buy a small piece of lean beef and make a pot roast. Often, though, for those occasions, I'll buy a duck. Duck has a lot of fat; my recipe eliminates a good bit of it, but not all. I also buy turkey quite often.

I use very little ground beef. Most often, I use ground veal, chicken, or turkey breast for my hamburgers. Sometimes I will buy a package of chicken cutlets and chop it up myself. It tastes best, but does take a little more work.

I try to cook as healthfully as possible and still enjoy the food. You can, too!

When I return from my Thursday shopping spree, I take out the products I plan to cook for Shabbos, like chicken and fish, and keep them in the refrigerator. I divide the rest into smaller packages for the freezer so that, when I want to cook just half a chicken, I don't have to defrost a whole one. Fish and ground meat get subdivided similarly.

About poultry

Of all the meats, chicken is one of the healthiest, according to the doctors. The breast portion, also called the white meat, is very lean, and is considered the healthiest part. The bottom of the chicken, also called the dark meat, although not as lean as the white meat, is still very much leaner than beef.

Many people feel that today's chickens are not as tasty as those of fifteen to twenty years ago, perhaps because chickens today are raised scientifically, with all kinds of injections, antibiotics, and medications to make them grow faster and bigger. In my opinion, the most important ingredient was removed — the taste. It is now up to the cook to give the chicken its taste by interesting seasoning. In the following pages, you will find many very good recipes that will make your chickens taste delicious.

The tastiest chicken is the one that you cook on the day that you buy it. While the chickens you put into your freezer are still good, freezing does take something away from the food. It dries out some of the fat, which contributes to the taste. On the other hand, frozen chickens and other meats that you put into your freezer will last a long time, and it's very convenient not to have to run to the butcher every time you want to cook!

One big improvement which today's chickens offer is the packaging. Chickens and chicken parts packaged on styrofoam or plastic trays, covered with clear plastic sealed at the seams, ensures that when people handle the meat packages at the store, they can see what they are getting without actually touching the meat itself.

When you buy your chickens, first look at the expiration date (which should be three days after the chicken was packaged), to be sure the package is fresh. Then look at the chicken itself. If you prefer a lean chicken, look for a bluish hue. I prefer the pale yellow chickens, even if a little more work is required to remove the chicken fat. Some people (including my own butcher) feel there is no difference in taste, but I have tried many and I feel that this chicken tastes better. The dark yellow ones have too much fat.

Mostly I buy whole chickens. I have sometimes found that, when you buy them in quarters, the butcher has packaged quarters from different chickens together. For instance, the tops can be light yellow, while the bottoms are bluish-white. When I buy a whole chicken, even though I have to cut the quarters myself, I know what I am getting. Some butchers will cut the chicken into quarters or eighths after you choose it whole.

Another good thing is that most butchers put a date on the label of the package and have an expiration date, three days after the packaging date. This way, you can tell if the chicken was packaged the day you bought it or the previous day and you can make sure that the meat is fresh.

Today, you can buy just the parts of the chicken that you like best. Breasts are often packaged together, and so are bottoms. You can buy the chicken whole, or cut into quarters or eighths, or chicken cutlets, which is the breast with all the bones removed. Your butcher can also grind the chicken for you, so that you can make patties or meat loaf, which are healthier than those made with beef. All the various options available make it easier to plan and prepare meals in small amounts, and to provide for people with varied preferences and taste.

The recipes on the following pages are for one chicken, or sometimes for half a chicken. If you cook only half of a chicken at a time, reduce the ingredients accordingly; if you cook more, increase them. Remember that most meats shrink during cooking — you may have only 75% or less of the original weight when you're done.

When buying chicken, you should buy the kind that is appropriate to what you want to cook. The younger the bird, the less time you need to cook it. If a young broiler is cooked too long, it will fall apart and lose some of its taste. Older birds need a longer time to finish cooking and are more appropriate for soup or for stewing.

It's advisable to plan what you want to prepare for side dishes. You may want a baked potato or sweet potato, which, depending on its size, could take at least an hour to bake in a conventional oven. By thinking ahead, you can put the washed potato into the oven (either wrapped in foil or just placed on the rack along with the chicken), and it will be ready at the same time as the chicken! You can also cook any other side dishes, timing things so that the whole meal is ready at the same time.

Both chicken and turkey taste best just out of the oven, so try to plan your cooking to be ready just at the time you want to have your meal.

If you have never cooked a chicken by yourself before, you may be afraid that the chicken will not taste good or that you will spoil it. Let me assure you that it is hard to spoil a chicken if it's fresh, whether just defrosted from the freezer or straight from the butcher shop. Let me also promise you that the chicken will be tasty and you will enjoy eating it! Just follow the instructions with each recipe, and pay particular attention to the section, *Seasoning the Food.*

Even though today's chickens are plucked and clean of feathers, they still need some cleaning, and quite often they have a lot of pin feathers that have to be removed. If you have a hard time with them, try soaking the chicken in hot water for two minutes, and they will come off much more easily. You can also use a strawberry huller or tweezers to pull out the pinfeathers.

The butcher usually leaves a lot of fat on. I remove this very carefully, because chicken fat is all cholesterol and can be hazardous to your (or at least, my) health! I take my time, doing a very thorough job. I even remove some of the fat under the skin, and I take off the tail, which is all fat, too.

Some people remove the skin altogether, to reduce the fat further, but I find that this makes the chicken too dry, especially the white meat, which is already a drier meat. Removing the skin works better with my *Best Southern Fried (Baked) Chicken*, since the breading keeps the chicken from drying out too much.

Some chickens come with the liver enclosed in

a plastic or special paper bag. Remember that the liver is not kosher unless specially prepared. (See *Appendix A*.) Be sure to remove it from the chicken before cooking!

The butcher may also enclose the neck and gizzard. I save these, putting them into a tightly closed plastic bag and freezing them. I cut the wings off and freeze them, too. I add to the bag every time I cook chicken, and when I have a large amount, I make *Chicken Fricassee*.

How do I know when the chicken is ready?

Some ovens, even when set for 350°F, may be hotter or cooler, so it may take a few minutes more or less than the recipe says, to cook your chicken. Therefore, you should check to see if it is ready. Normally, a four-pound chicken should be ready in 1½ to 1¾ hours, so check it after about one hour and ten minutes.

Pierce the bottom, near the thigh, with a fork. If the juice is clear, the chicken is done. If it's red or pink, it's not done yet. Or, you can remove a small piece of meat near the thigh and taste it.

If you are in a hurry, you can increase the oven temperature by 25°. At 350°F to 375°F, a 3½-pound broiler should only take 1 to 1½ hours to be ready.

About meat

Everybody knows today that consuming too much red meat can be detrimental to your health. Beef has a lot of fat, which can clog up your arteries. Many people, though, do not pay much attention to the dangers of fat in meats, until their doctors warn them to stop eating red meat because their cholesterol has reached a dangerous level. Even so, some people will still indulge in beef meals occasionally. After all, good roast beef, with a tasty gravy, mashed potatoes, asparagus, and carrots, is still a very tempting meal. I personally treat myself to this delicious meal a few times a year, for very special occasions. I have therefore included a number of very good recipes for beef and veal.

Fat in the meat

There is no question that fat in chickens and any other meats, beef and veal included, enhances their flavor. However, you have to decide if the difference in the taste is worth the additional amount of cholesterol that the fat adds to the meal.

To reduce the hazard of the fat in beef, cut off most of the fat before cooking. You'll never get all of the fat in beef, for instance, because the fat is also deep inside the meat. There remains enough fat between the fibers of the meat to give it taste. Therefore, the gravy produced in cooking gives the meat and potatoes that special, good flavor.

To help reduce fat and cholesterol, I use a Gravy Skimmer™ to remove harmful fat from the meat gravy after the meat is cooked. Another method is to chill the gravy or soup by leaving it in the refrigerator after it's cooked and cooled off. It is then easy to remove the layer of fat which solidifies at the top.

The cuts of beef that I like to use are brisket, shell roast, silver tip roast, and side of steak roast. Some butchers have different names for them. Therefore ask your butcher what he calls the leanest cuts of beef. While veal, too, has fat, doctors and nutritionists seem to favor it over beef. Still, do remove as much of the fat as you can, as you do with beef. You should also balance your meals by including a lot of fresh salads and cooked vegetables in your menus. Any roast can be cooked with a few potatoes, peeled and cut into halves or quarters, and added to the sauce for 25-35 minutes (not longer, as potatoes will fall apart). Potatoes absorb the juice of the meat, giving them a very tasty flavor. You may need to add a little more water to the pot during cooking.

HOW TO
BUY FISH

*Nutritionists and doctors tell us
that fish is healthier than any meat,
and they recommend having fish for dinner
several times a week.
There are many types of kosher fish to choose from
and most are easy to prepare and cook quickly.*

♦   ♦   ♦   ♦   ♦   ♦   ♦   ♦   ♦

In order for a fish to be considered kosher, it must have both fins and scales. We are not allowed to eat any shellfish, like oysters, shrimp, lobster, clams, crabs, snails, or any scavenger fish.

Serving fish on Shabbos and Jewish holidays has been a tradition for centuries. Carp, whitefish, and yellow pike are customary. I also cook whiting, if I can get large ones. They are all cooked in the same way, and make a very tasty sauce when boiled. Carp, whitefish, and pike have very small bones in the tail and the fleshy part of the meat. Be very careful when you eat them!

Traditional Shabbos fish usually has a jelled sauce. Some fish jell more easily than others. The sauce from any carp will jell in the refrigerator, if you don't use too much water in the cooking, and so will the sauce from whiting. Boiling the head of the fish along with the slices will help jell the sauce.

I use a 7" round x 3" deep pot to boil my fish. This size is just big enough to boil four pieces of fish. For whitefish, I use about 2½ cups of water, plus the other ingredients in the recipe. The water just barely covers the fish. After cooking, I end up

with 1¼-1½ cups of sauce that will jell if left overnight in the refrigerator. With other fish, such as carp, pike, and whiting, I use about 3 cups of water, plus the other ingredients, and end up with about 2 cups of jelled sauce.

Some fish take less time to cook than others. Winter carp, or white carp, takes fifteen minutes less time to cook than regular carp. If cooked too long, all fish will fall apart; therefore you have to check it frequently.

Then, of course, there is the famous *gefilte fish*, which is often made of a combination of two or three of the different kinds of fish mentioned above. The fish are ground and then mixed together and made into balls. (See recipe on the following pages.)

There are two kinds of carp that I use. One is the regular carp, which is usually from Michigan. They are raised in artificial fish ponds, but don't taste as good as did the carp of fifteen or twenty years ago, which were natural. The polluted waters, too, are somewhat to blame for the taste. The Michigan carp is quite large and fat, dark in color, and not too tasty. The male has milt, which tastes like liver. The female is slightly lighter in color, tastes a little bit better, and has roe, which is very tasty, but unfortunately high in cholesterol. I always tell the man at the fish store to throw it away. If I take it home, I know I will cook it — this way I am not tempted. This carp works fairly well for gefilte fish.

Winter, or white, carp is also large, with slightly less fat. The meat is white and tastes a lot better than that of the regular carp. I boil this fish. Most fish stores sell both kinds of carp, either whole or cleaned and sliced (at a higher price). Tell them to cut your fish into one-inch (1") slices — I find that they taste better than two-inch (2") slices.

In the winter, since you can't always get the fish you want, you may decide to buy a larger quantity when it is available. When you come home from the store, wash and dry it, and then separate the slices, three or four to a package, and freeze them. This way you don't have to defrost a whole fish when you want only a portion or two. Freezing the fish will dry out some of the fat and the meat, so it will lose a little of the taste, but the slices will last a long time in the freezer (six months or longer), if frozen solid. Never refreeze any fish that has already defrosted!

Then there are whitefish and pike. They have drier meat, are softer, and take only a few minutes to cook. I personally prefer the taste of these fish. Have these sliced in 1½" slices — no smaller, or they will fall apart in cooking.

Whiting usually comes in small sizes, but larger ones are sometimes available, too. This is also a soft fish and has to be cooked very gently. Have it cut in 2½" widths, making about two to three slices per fish, depending on the size. Whiting has a large center bone. The rest of the meat is smooth and has very few bones. I cook the whiting the same way as I cook carp. Before cooking, remove the dark inside membrane (skin-like layer). Otherwise, it will adhere to the meat and will be very hard to remove later. Whiting can also be bought filleted and may be cooked the same way as other fillets: broiled, fried, or baked.

For everyday use, there are quite a few kosher fish to choose from. I use flounder, trout, red snapper, sole, halibut, cod, tile fish, and salmon. The last four I buy in steak cuts, as well as filleted.

These fish can be broiled, baked, poached, or fried. My recipes call for cooking them in various ways, depending on the type of fish. Flounder and trout can also be bought whole and are suitable for baking, broiling, or frying. Salmon should be dark red in color to taste the best. The best salmon is from Norway.

When you buy any whole fish, look at the eyes. If they are clear and bulging, it usually means that the fish is fresh. The meat of flounder, cod, halibut, and tile fish should be very white in color. When the meat is slightly tan or grey, it means that it has been in the display case for awhile. It will not harm you, but it will not taste as good. Just like we say regarding meat: the fresher, the tastier.

Fish goes well with a fresh vegetable salad and cooked vegetables, like broccoli, potatoes, cauliflower, sweet peas, or carrots. See recipes in the *Vegetables* chapter.

HOME FROM THE
MARKET

♦　♦　♦　♦　♦　♦　♦　♦　♦

Now that we've done our shopping for the weekend, let's unpack the groceries. We'll save the big plastic bags and use them as garbage can liners. We'll also keep a few of the plastic vegetable bags and twist ties to use for bagging things for the freezer.

Now. What goes where?

First we take the string beans out of the plastic bag and transfer them to a paper bag. Since string beans spoil very quickly, they will develop brown spots and spoil in a few (2-3) days if they have no air. In a paper bag, they will last for five or six days.

Next, we put the celery into a plastic bag. This keeps it crisp and fresh. Every time we use some of the celery, we will wipe the remaining stalks with a paper towel, wrap them in a dry paper towel, and then put it all back into the plastic bag. This makes celery last twice as long and keeps it crisp and dry. We do the same with the carrots.

We put the hard green or brown pears into a glass dish and leave them out on the counter for a few days until they start to get a little riper. We do the same with the hard tomatoes. Remember, though, when we picked the tomatoes at the store, we took one or two slightly softer ones to use today or tomorrow in our salad. These should go into the refrigerator.

We put avocado into the same dish as the pears. It may take as much as five days to ripen. We'll test the avocado by pressing on the skin. When there is a slight give, it's ready, and it will keep in the refrigerator up to five or more days. Once you start using it, sprinkle some lemon juice on the cut edge to keep it from discoloring. Also leave the pit inside, and wrap the whole avocado tightly in aluminum foil.

The cantaloupe and melons should also stay on the counter for a few days until they ripen, depending on how they are when you bring them home. Sometimes they can take as much as a week or even longer to ripen. Bananas, too, stay on the counter. All other fruits and most vegetables go into the vegetable bins in the refrigerator.

We keep potatoes and onions in the bottom of a kitchen cabinet. Neither needs refrigeration, and the onions' odor could get into other foods stored nearby in the enclosed environment of a refrigerator. Don't keep onions in a plastic bag — they will spoil very fast. They usually come in a net, designed to let air circulate. The potatoes may keep as long as a month, the onions for about three weeks.

Now let's take care of the fish. Take the carp and wash it well, and then we'll take out the portions we want to cook for the weekend. We divide up the rest of the fish into packages containing as many pieces as we might need each time. (I usually pack three or four slices per package.) We then put these packages into plastic bags, close them tightly with twist ties, and freeze them.

We'll put all of the chickens into the freezer, except those that we need for the weekend, which we will keep in the refrigerator. It's also a good idea to divide some of the bottoms of the chicken (the thighs), which come four in a package. I like to put two in each plastic bag. That way, I can take out and defrost enough for about two days. Cooked chicken tastes best the first two days; after that, it may lose a little of its taste. If you bought any ground meat, you may want to divide it into two or more portions for different meals, depending on how much was in the package. It's a good idea to label each package as to its contents and date of purchase. Be sure to use the oldest products first.

Ready to Cook Your First Meal?

READY TO COOK YOUR FIRST MEAL?

Well, you've learned how to shop
for fruits and vegetables, poultry, meat, and fish.
You know how to store everything
once you get it home.
You even know how to prepare
a lot of different recipes.
Now, it's time to make a whole meal.
It can be hard at first, but I'll be here to help,
and with a little guidance from me and a little practice,
you'll be fine!

♦　♦　♦　♦　♦　♦　♦　♦　♦

How to Time Your Preparations

You can actually start on your dinner preparations in the morning. Suppose you want to cook chicken. What I do is clean the chicken in the morning, season it, then put it in into the baking dish and leave it in the refrigerator for the rest of the day, covered with foil. Then I go to work or do whatever I have to do.

Chicken tastes best just out of the oven. If I want to eat at 6:00 PM, I start cooking the chicken so that it will be out of the oven at just about that time. Say my recipe tells me it will take 1½ hours to cook or bake the chicken. I will heat the oven at 4:10 and put the chicken in at about 4:15 or 4:20. The chicken will be cooked and ready to eat at just the right time.

If I have to prepare any side dishes or salads, I do that during the day, or I make enough for a few days when I cook. Even a salad of lettuce and other vegetables can be left over for the next day as long as you don't put any dressing on it and you take the tomato out, since it is too moist. Cover the glass dish with plastic wrap, making sure that it's airtight. This keeps the lettuce from getting soft and wilting. The lettuce will then stay crisp and fresh for another day.

Cooked side dishes can be kept in the refrigerator for a few days and will taste as good as the first day. Just add a little water and stir while you warm it over a low flame.

Let's Get Started

If you like, put on your new rubber gloves when handling fish and meat products. Take the chicken out of the plastic bag, wash it off, and dry it with a paper towel. Now take an 8" pointed knife and remove all the chicken fat you can. Lift up the skin wherever you can and get that fat, too. Whatever is white or yellow should come off. Then we'll look for pinfeathers, and pluck them off as much as possible. The stubborn ones usually come out more easily if you let the chicken stay a few minutes in hot water.

Now it's time to season the chicken, but you first have to decide how you want to cook it. Look through the many recipes I've given you in the chapter on *Poultry Dishes,* and follow the one you choose.

While the chicken is cooking, you may want to prepare some side dishes. Look in the *Side Dishes* and *Vegetable Dishes* chapters and choose one or two from each, as well.

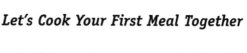

Let's Cook Your First Meal Together

After looking in the chapter called *Poultry Dishes*, let's say you selected *Baked Chicken*, to be accompanied by baked potato, carrots, a salad, some fresh fruit for dessert, and a cup of tea.

Now let's work together. Since you are only one for dinner, we will bake only half a chicken — this will be enough for two days. If you want more, all you have to do is put up the whole chicken, the same way.

You have already cleaned the chicken, so let us heat the oven to 350°F while we season the chicken. We will put a piece of foil into an eight-inch (8") metal baking pan. Lining the pan like this makes it very easy to clean it after the chicken is baked.

We place two quarters of chicken, one top (breast) and one bottom (thigh), skin-side down, on the foil. We rub the chicken with a little Italian dressing, and then we sprinkle it with a little less than half a teaspoon of salt, just a light dusting. Now, we shake a pinch or two of pepper on each quarter. After this, it's the garlic powder's turn — be a little more generous and sprinkle enough to cover the chicken pieces. To give it a little color, we'll also dust them with a little paprika, lightly.

Let's turn the chicken skin-side up and do the same thing on the skin that we did on the back side. You can move the skin away and dust the meat with the seasoning, and then cover it again with the skin.

By now the oven is hot, and we put the baking pan, covered with a sheet of foil, in the center of the oven. We will also wash a potato, pierce it, and put it on the oven rack to bake at the same time.

Mark down on a piece of paper what time you put up the chicken, so you can tell when it should be ready. After baking for 20 minutes, take off the foil cover.

While the chicken is baking, let's peel four or five carrots, slice them, and put them into a small pot with enough water to almost cover them. Cover the pot but leave the lid a little askew, so that the steam can escape, and start to cook it over a medium flame. After ten minutes, we check the carrots — since they are not sweet, we add one teaspoon of honey. That should do it — if not, add more.

Let the carrots simmer another five to ten minutes, but watch out — sometimes the water boils out sooner and the carrots get burned, so check every few minutes, adding water if needed.

Let's look in on the chicken. It smells delicious! Use the quilted gloves, since the dish is piping hot. Take the pan from the oven and place it on a heat-proof surface. Baste the chicken, spooning the juices from the pan over the chicken pieces. If there's not enough liquid, add a little hot water or orange juice (about ¼ cup) to the pan. Now put the pan back into the oven, uncovered.

How about making a salad? We take off a few leaves from a head of lettuce, wash them well, dry them well in a paper towel, and tear them into smaller pieces, putting them into a glass dish. *(Don't cut the lettuce with a knife — the edges will turn brown that way.)* Then cut a few slices of tomato and cut them into smaller pieces, also. Now we'll wash a cucumber and do the same thing. Cover the glass dish with plastic wrap, really well so that it's airtight, and let it chill in the refrigerator.

How's our chicken coming? Let's take it out

and baste it again. It looks very nice and crisp. We will turn it over and let the other side get brown, too. Baste it again; then back it goes into the oven. If the chicken gets too dark, but it's not done yet, cover the baking pan with the foil again.

Now you have just enough time to set the table. Put down a large dinner plate. On the left side of the plate goes the folded napkin. Put the fork on the napkin. (Some people place the napkin on the dinner plate, if there is no dish with an appetizer on it.) On the right side of the dinner plate goes the knife, and then the soup spoon. Place a drinking glass on the right side, above the knife and spoon. When setting for company, salt and pepper shakers as well as the bread basket should go in the middle of the table so that they can be reached, or easily passed, by each guest.

How about an appetizer? Let's cut a pink grapefruit in half, section it, put it onto a small plate, and place it on the dinner plate.

The chicken is now ready. It took only an hour and fifteen minutes. The grapefruit is sour? Well, sprinkle a little sugar on it. Did you say the chicken is delicious and so is the potato? Oh, and the carrots are also tasty? Well, didn't I tell you you'd have a delicious meal? Everything worked out fine. The salad is nice and crisp, too.

You are happy, and so am I. Don't forget the fresh pear for dessert. Do you still want tea? Just boil some water and dip in the tea bag for a few seconds, depending on how strong you like it. Sugar? You don't take sugar; that's smart.

'Bye now. I have to go home and cook my own dinner!

Vegetables

Handling and Preparation

Potatoes, Plain and Fancy

Vegetable Dishes

VEGETABLES: HANDLING AND PREPARATION

♦　　♦　　♦　　♦　　♦　　♦　　♦　　♦　　♦

Onions: The onion is one of the most important vegetables used in cooking. It is an essential ingredient in soups, appetizers, main courses, and side dishes. Sometimes it's used whole, but more often it's sliced or diced — so every cook needs to know how to peel and chop an onion.

Of course, there are other vegetables and fruits that also have to be peeled or sliced before using. Later in this chapter, I will discuss peeling and cutting some of those other vegetables. It's really not difficult and you will find that your skill will increase with practice.

Onions, however, present a unique problem, because the vapor (especially from the common yellow onion) is very strong and makes most people "cry" while peeling them. Some people advised me to work with the onion near the sink and let the water run while peeling or chopping it. Others told me to let the water run on the onion while working with it. I have tried both methods, and neither has worked for me. My eyes still tear when I'm peeling an onion.

I have also tried to chop an onion with a plastic onion chopper, which encloses the onion while chopping it, but it takes quite a long time to chop even a small onion. I therefore find it impractical.

I've recently been told about a method that might really work. Peel and chop onions while breathing *only* through your mouth. The tearing seems to be associated with the nose, so if you don't inhale — even slightly — you should be okay. It's certainly worth a try!

Still, there are a few different kinds of onions that are much milder and will make your eyes tear less. The Vidalia onion is very mild and sweet and it will not make you tear too much. However, it is only on the market in the spring for a few months. There are also the Spanish onion, the Bermuda onion, and the white onion, which are all milder than the regular yellow onion.

To peel an onion, first cut off both ends, then peel off and discard the outermost layers of skin. If you want to slice the onion into rings, cut the onion through the width, in the thickness you desire. To chop, cut the peeled onion in half, place it on your cutting board and cut through the onion in the length, then in the width. You may then have pieces that are too large for your purpose. Transfer the cut onion to your chopping bowl and continue to chop until you have the size you want.

The vegetable peeler and how to use it

The vegetable peeler used to be called the potato peeler, until it was given a lot more responsibility and someone changed its name to "vegetable peeler." It is probably one of the most important small kitchen tools ever invented. (See *Appendix C* on *Kitchen Tools and Gadgets* for a picture of one.)

Potatoes: If you have never peeled a potato before, or if you have little experience, peeling a few potatoes for practice, along with a little patience, will give you the skill and speed to peel a potato or any other peelable vegetable or fruit.

The potato peeler is designed to cut the peel and not to cut off too much of the potato. Unlike the small paring knife, which was used for this purpose before the vegetable peeler was invented, the peeler does not cut off a thick layer of the potato with the peel.

I always wear rubber gloves while peeling, especially potatoes, because the soil (dirt) gets into your skin, even if you wash the potato first. You can't get it out unless you wash your hands many times. The rubber gloves prevent this problem.

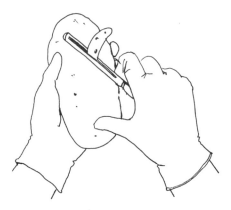

If you are right-handed, hold the potato with the width, or thick side, facing you, in your left hand. (If you are left-handed, do the reverse.) Take the peeler in your right hand, and, with a little pressure toward the potato, move the peeler from the top downward. Move the potato up and cut down again, until you have cut all the way around the potato. now move the potato, still in your left hand, so that the flat side of the potato faces you. Cut the peel from the top downward, strip after strip, until that side is completely peeled. Turn the potato and peel the other side the same way.

You may still have to cut out some eyelets with

the tip of the peeler or a sharp knife. Then wash the potatoes and slice them as you wish. If you are not using them immediately, it is advisable to put the peeled potatoes into a dish of cold water, to prevent discoloring.

For long vegetables, like cucumbers or carrots, trim the ends, peel half way, then turn and peel the other half. Always peel from the top downward, to keep the peels from flying all over the place.

Carrots: Cut off both ends, then peel the carrot with a vegetable peeler. You can cut the carrot in rounds or in long "sticks," according to your taste. When cutting rounds, I sometimes slice more than one carrot at a time, using a longer knife and cutting across two or three carrots at the same time, in the desired thickness. This reduces the preparation time.

Celery: Wash thoroughly, cut off ends, and slice to the desired thickness, cut into "sticks," or dice.

Cucumbers: These can be prepared in two ways. You can peel the cucumber first, before slicing it into the desired thicknesses. Or, as some people do, leave the peel on, wash the cucumber very thoroughly, cut the ends off and discard them, then slice it in the desired thickness. Just like carrots, cucumbers can be sliced in "rounds" or in "sticks," whichever you prefer.

Radishes: Wash and cut off a very small piece from each end, then slice each radish in thin slices.

Tomatoes: Wash tomatoes thoroughly. Remove the end where the root grew, and slice through the width. To remove the skin of a tomato:

Use a sharp knife to make some small cuts in the skin. Put the ripe tomato into boiling water for 10 seconds. Remove and peel. If done properly, the skin should come off easily.

Sautéing Onions and Other Vegetables

Slice or mince the vegetable. Heat the frying pan and melt 2-3 Tbs. margarine in it, or heat 2-3 Tbs. vegetable oil in the pan. The hot oil will help to prevent the vegetables from sticking. Reduce flame, add the vegetable, and fry lightly ("sauté") until golden, stirring often to prevent burning. Add more oil or margarine as needed.

Use this method to prepare sautéed onions, garlic, mushrooms, tomatoes, or any other vegetable.

When sautéing onions, you can also cover the frying pan with a tight-fitting lid, reduce the flame, and sauté them for 3-5 minutes. This will make the onions more golden, since the cover adds moisture and prevents burning.

Hints & Tips

See Appendix B on how to inspect vegetables for insect infestation and how to clean them before use.

	Raw	**Cooked**
Asparagus*	Not used in raw state.	Cut off the white ends — they will not get soft no matter how long you cook them. Place asparagus into a large pot of boiling salted water, reduce to medium flame. Boil 8-10 minutes. Drain. Serve with *White Sauce* or *Cheese Sauce* for a dairy meal.
Avocado	Best served cut open and raw, with a little salt. Also, mixed into salads.	Seldom used cooked.
Beets	Not served raw.	Clean beets and cut off stems and leaves. Peel and cut into slices. Boil in water to cover at least 45 minutes, or longer (young beets take only 40 minutes; older ones can take 1½ hours or longer). Drain and season to taste.
Broccoli*	Clean. Remove leaves and trim bottom of stem. Cut florets off at base and serve in salad or as crudités. Stalks can be munched or cooked.	With a sharp knife, remove the first layer of skin off the stem and slice off bottom of stem. Remove leaves and cut florets into smaller pieces. Steam for 6-12 minutes. Or boil in enough water to cover vegetables halfway. Add salt, if desired. Cook for 10-12 minutes. Drain. Season to taste. Good with a sauce. See also: *Broccoli Soufflé* in this chapter.
Brussels Sprouts*	Not used in raw state.	Remove wilted leaves, cut off stems. Soak 10 minutes in cold water. Boil in a small amount of salted water, about 10-15 minutes, or steam, until soft. Season to taste. Excellent with *White Sauce*.
Cabbage* **White and Purple**	Trim off wilted or brown spots. Shred by hand or in food processor. Make into cole slaw.	Clean as for serving raw. Use in stuffed cabbage, cooked in sweet and sour tomato sauce, or cooked and mixed with cooked noodles.
Carrots	Peel or scrape, cut off ends, cut in half or quarters lengthwise, then cut into 4-5" strips, enjoy! Or slice or dice into salads.	Keep in mind that baby carrots take longer to cook than the large carrots. After cleaning, slice, put into water, and boil or steam for at least 8-20 minutes, or until soft. See also: Various carrot dishes later in this chapter.

*Note: Should be carefully checked for the presence of insects, according to the guidelines listed in Appendix B.

	Raw	**Cooked**
Cauliflower*	Remove leaves; cut off any black spots; cut into florets, cut in half. Discard stem. Serve in salad or as crudités.	Clean as for raw serving. Steam or boil in a little water for 10-15 minutes. Do not overcook. Good with *White Sauce*. See also: *Cauliflower Croquettes*.
Celery*	Same as for *carrots*. Leaves should be discarded, or carefully checked before using.	Add to soups, fish, salads.
Corn*	Not used in raw state.	Pull off husk and silk and rinse. Boil, covered, in vigorously boiling water, 3-4 minutes for young corn, 5-6 minutes for older, or until soft. Good with butter and a little salt.
Cucumbers	Wash thoroughly or peel, then slice into salads.	Seldom used cooked.
Eggplant	Never used raw.	See recipes later in this chapter.
Garlic	Separate cloves and peel. Mince and add to salads.	Press in a garlic press or mince. Add to meat dishes, soups, and roasts.
Lettuce*	Remove wilted or brown-spotted leaves. Take as many leaves as you will need for your salad. Wash carefully, dry, and wrap in a paper towel. Return to plastic bag, closing tightly.	Seldom used cooked.
Okra	Not used in raw state.	Wash, cut off ends, and either slice or cook whole. Use in soup or boil separately (about 10 minutes uncut, 5-6 minutes sliced), season to taste. *White Sauce* is a good addition.

* Note: Should be carefully checked for the presence of insects, according to the guidelines listed in Appendix B.

	Raw	**Cooked**
Onions	Slice off top and bottom. Peel off outer layer. Slice or dice into salads.	Peel and add to many recipes, whole, sliced, or diced.
Peppers **Red and Green** **Sweet (Bell)**	Clean thoroughly, removing stem and insides. (Many people are highly allergic to the seeds.) Slice or dice into salads.	Can be added to many dishes as major ingredient or as a garnish. See recipes.
Potatoes	Not used raw.	Vegetable most commonly used as a side dish. Wash potatoes thoroughly before cooking. May be cooked in or out of peel. To boil, peel potatoes, cut into quarters, put into a pot of water (perhaps with 1 tsp. of salt) and boil 20-25 minutes. See also: section on *Potatoes*.
Radishes	Trim tops and bottoms, clean thoroughly and slice into salads.	Seldom used cooked.
Scallions* **(Green Onion)**	Use in salads, or diced and mixed into cream or cottage cheese.	Can be used as ingredient in recipes and cooked or sautéed along with other vegetables.
Spinach*	Remove stems and clean leaves thoroughly. Can be tossed into salads.	Steam or boil briefly, until soft, or chop and sauté with onion and garlic.
String Beans **(Green Beans)**	Can be used raw on a vegetable platter with a dip. Wash and cut off ends before serving.	Cut ends off and wash beans. Steam for 10 minutes, or boil in enough salted water to cover, for 15-18 minutes. Rinse in cold water. Drain. Add margarine, salt and/or pepper, to taste. Can also be sautéed for a few minutes in margarine. Serve immediately.

* Note: Should be carefully checked for the presence of insects, according to the guidelines listed in Appendix B.

	Raw	Cooked
Sweet Potatoes & Yams	Never used raw.	Wash and dry on a paper towel. Do not peel. They can be boiled, but are best baked, depending on size, 1 hour or more — the longer the better. Do not under-bake. They should be very soft. Cut into slices 1" wide or serve whole. See recipes.
Tomatoes	Wash and slice.	Sometimes used in sauces, soups, and other recipes.
Zucchini	Usually cooked. Can also be sliced raw into salads or used as crudités.	Wash thoroughly. Cut off ends, but do not peel. Slice into 3/4" slices. Dust lightly on both sides with salt, pepper and/or garlic powder (to taste). Dip into flour. Fry until edges turn golden brown. Turn and fry other side. Place on a paper towel to absorb oil. See also: *Zucchini & Vegetables*, below.

*Note: Should be carefully checked for the presence of insects, according to the guidelines listed in Appendix B.

POTATOES,
PLAIN AND FANCY

Potatoes are such a versatile vegetable,
they deserve a section of their own.
They can be used peeled or unpeeled,
boiled and eaten plain,
mashed or fried, made into salads, baked in kugels,
or baked whole and eaten as they are
with a variety of toppings.
Potatoes can serve as a side dish or even
as a hearty main course.
From among these recipes, choose the ones
that fit your menu and your appetite.

♦   ♦   ♦   ♦   ♦   ♦   ♦   ♦   ♦

Baked Potatoes

1 Wash as many potatoes as you need — one per serving. Dry with a paper towel.

2 Pierce each potato with a fork in a few places, to keep it from bursting in the oven.

3 Place them on baking rack in the oven at 400°F, and bake 45 minutes to 1 hour, or until soft.

To bake a potato in a microwave oven, prepare it as you would for conventional baking. Place it into the microwave and bake it on high power for 4-6 minutes, depending on the size of the potato. When baking more than one at a time, add 2 minutes for each additional potato.

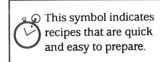 This symbol indicates recipes that are quick and easy to prepare.

Baked Potatoes with Vegetables

4 large baking potatoes
(or more)

1 small onion

¼ - ⅓ of a small can of
sliced mushrooms
or 5 oz. fresh mushrooms

⅓ can of small sweet peas
or ¼ - ⅓ of a 10-oz. box
frozen peas

2 Tbs. margarine, or more

⅛ - ¼ cup parve
coffee creamer,
or milk for dairy use

½ tsp. salt

Pepper to taste

Oil for sautéing

1 Wash one potato per serving and dry in a paper towel. Pierce each potato with a fork in a few places.

2 Bake at 375°-400° for 35-40 minutes.

3 While potatoes are baking, cut onions and mushrooms into small pieces, and sauté them in oil.

4 Boil frozen peas as directed on package and set aside, or just add canned peas when making mixture.

5 After potatoes have baked for 35-40 minutes, take them out of the oven and cut off ¼ of each potato, lengthwise. Remove pulp from potatoes and tops. Place into a dish and mash with a potato masher or a fork, adding margarine and parve coffee creamer or milk, a little at a time. Mix well until very smooth.

6 Add onions, mushrooms, and peas. Season to taste. Mix very well.

7 Put mixture back into shells. Cover with tops, return to oven on a baking sheet, and bake another 10-15 minutes at 350°F. Serve hot.

To keep potatoes hot, shut off oven, wrap each potato separately in foil, and leave in oven.

Fried Red Potatoes

This is a delicious dish, and it only takes thirty minutes to prepare and cook.

Use only red potatoes. In my experience, this recipe will not work with any other kind.

1 Peel potatoes and cut into chunks about 1"-1¼" in length (like French fries but twice as thick and half as long).

2 Chop onion into medium-size pieces and, in a large skillet or frying pan, sauté in oil for a few minutes.

3 Add potatoes, more oil, and salt and pepper to taste. Dust with paprika.

4 Reduce heat to a very low simmer. Cover pan. Let cook 15-18 minutes, stirring and mixing onions and potatoes frequently, so that they do not stick to the frying pan. Check every 5 minutes, adding oil when needed.

Dish is ready when potatoes are soft enough to eat and are browned. Serve hot.

3-4 red-skinned potatoes

1 medium Spanish or white onion

Oil to fry

½-1 tsp. salt or to taste

2-3 dashes pepper

½-¾ tsp. paprika

Hints & Tips

Refrigerate any leftover Fried Red Potatoes and reheat them the next day in a frying pan with additional oil, stirring frequently.

Mashed (or Boiled) Potatoes

3 large potatoes
*Russet potatoes are best
for this recipe*

**2-3 Tbs. margarine
or butter (for dairy)**

**¼ cup warmed parve
coffee creamer or milk
(for dairy)**

½ tsp. salt, or to taste

Dash pepper, or to taste

*This recipe is for 2 portions — for more, increase
ingredients proportionately.*

1 Peel and slice potatoes and put into pot. Fill
with enough water to cover and boil for 15-20
minutes or until soft.

2 Drain the water.

*At this point you can eat the boiled potatoes with
a little salt and pepper, or you can go on to mash
them.*

3 Mash potatoes and margarine or butter with a
potato masher or a fork.

4 Add warmed creamer or milk. Mash and mix
until very smooth. Add more margarine and
creamer, if needed. Season to taste with salt and
pepper. Serve immediately, *hot.*

*You can also mix in chopped, sautéed onions.
(See How to Sauté Vegetables, page 32.)*

Potatoes and Eggs

This makes a delicious side dish or a very quick and tasty snack.

2-3 large potatoes

1-2 eggs

Salt and pepper to taste

1 Peel 2-3 large potatoes, and follow the recipe for *Mashed Potatoes* from the previous page.

2 Boil 1-2 eggs for about 4-5 minutes. Remove the soft-boiled eggs from their shells and pour over mashed potatoes. Add salt and pepper. Mix well.

This same dish can also be made with a fried egg served over the mashed potatoes. It may not be as healthy because of frying the egg, but it is very tasty! Place hot mashed potatoes on each person's plate and top them with a fried egg. Season to taste. Mix them together as you eat.

Potato Pudding Soufflé

1 Peel, cook, and mash potatoes (see recipe above for *Mashed Potatoes*).

5 large potatoes

4 eggs

2 tsp. salt

Pepper to taste

½ stick margarine

1-1½ small onions

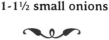

2 Separate eggs (see page 36); add beaten egg yolks to potatoes and season to taste with salt and pepper.

3 Chop the onions finely; add them and the margarine to the potato mixture. Mix until smooth.

4 Beat egg whites until stiff peaks form. Fold into potato mixture.

4 Put into well-greased oven-proof baking dish. Bake at 400°F for about 45 minutes or until slightly brown on top. Serve immediately.

Best Potato Salad

4 large Idaho potatoes

1 large carrot

1½ stalks celery

¾ sweet onion
(white, Vidalia, or Spanish)

1 half-sour or sour pickle

2 hard-boiled eggs

1 tsp. salt, or to taste

Dash or two of pepper,
to taste

½ - ¾ tsp. of sugar
(optional)

1 Tbs. vinegar, or to taste

¼ - ½ cup mayonnaise

It's really delicious!

1 Peel potatoes and cook in a large pot of water until done but still firm, about 10-14 minutes.

2 Drain. Cut potatoes into ¾" chunks.

3 Grate carrot coarsely on a hand-held grater or in food processor; sprinkle grated carrot over potatoes.

4 Slice celery into ½" slices. Dice onions, pickle, and eggs, and add them all to the potato mixture.

5 Add salt, pepper, sugar, vinegar, and enough mayonnaise to make it smooth. Mix everything together well.

Refrigerate for 2 hours or overnight. Serve cold.

Baked Dilled Potatoes

This delicious side dish is very easy to make, and your guests will love it.

1 Preheat oven to 375-400°.

2 Peel potatoes (one per serving), and cut into 1" chunks. Wash and dry in a paper towel.

3 In a large bowl, mix potatoes with the olive oil until well covered.

4 Sprinkle with dried or freshly chopped dill. Season with salt and pepper to taste and mix again. Then sprinkle lightly with a small amount of paprika (about ¼ tsp.). Mix again and spread on a greased baking sheet.

5 Place into preheated oven and bake 20 minutes. Turn potatoes over with a spatula and bake 20 minutes more, or until crisp and lightly browned.

Drain off excess oil on a paper towel. Serve hot. *You may want to add more salt and pepper to taste.*

2 or more large Idaho potatoes

2 Tbs. olive oil

½ - 1 tsp. dried dill
(or fresh, chopped)

Salt and pepper to taste

¼ - ½ tsp. paprika

French "Fried" Potatoes

3-4 Idaho potatoes

3-4 Tbs. melted
margarine or vegetable oil

Salt and pepper to taste

These potatoes are baked instead of deep fried in oil, so they are much healthier.

1 Preheat oven to 400°.

2 Peel and wash potatoes, and cut them lengthwise into ½" strips.

3 Drizzle melted margarine or vegetable oil over potato strips, coating well. You might use a vegetable brush for this.

4 Spread potatoes on a greased baking sheet. Season with salt and pepper to taste. Bake in preheated oven for 35-45 minutes until golden brown.

Turn potatoes after 20 minutes. Check and mix frequently, so that potatoes do not burn or stick to the pan.

When done, spread on a paper towel to absorb oil. Serve hot. *Good with tomato ketchup.*

Potato Pancakes (Latkes)

This recipe will make enough for 3-4 good-sized portions.

4-5 large Idaho potatoes
or other white potatoes

1 Peel and grate potatoes and onions by hand or in food processor. Combine with egg, if using, flour, salt, and pepper. If mixture becomes watery, pour a little water off, but leave some in.

1 egg
(optional)

**2-3 Tbs. flour
or matzah meal**

¾-1 tsp. salt

2 Heat frying pan with 2 Tbs. oil. Then reduce heat to medium-low. Spoon in about 1½-2 Tbs. of the mixture and, using a large spoon, form round or oval shapes.

Dash of pepper

½ small onion

Oil for frying

3 Fry 3 or 4 pancakes at the same time. When lightly browned, turn and fry other side. Place on a paper towel to absorb oil. Serve hot.

Some people eat potato pancakes with apple-sauce; others like sour cream. I like them dunked into a good meat sauce.

Potato Pancakes from Cooked Potatoes

This is a different kind of pancake — very tasty!

4-5 large Idaho potatoes

3-4 eggs

1-1½ tsp. salt, or to taste

Dash of pepper, or to taste

2-3 Tbs. parve creamer or milk for dairy
(optional)

1 Peel and cook potatoes for 12-14 minutes until soft, but still firm. Drain and let cool for 10 minutes.

2 Grate on hand-held potato grater, using the large holes, or in food processor.

3 Separate eggs (see page 36). Add egg yolks, salt and pepper to taste, and milk or parve creamer. Mix well until smooth, using potato masher or electric mixer.

4 Beat egg whites with electric mixer until stiff peaks form. Fold into mixture.

5 Heat frying pan with 2-3 Tbs. vegetable oil. Reduce heat to medium-low. Drop large spoonfuls of the mixture into the frying pan, using the spoon to form oval or round pancakes, about ⅓" thick.

6 Fry about 4 at a time. Let brown, then turn and brown other side. Add more oil as needed. This recipe requires a lot of oil.

When pancakes are fried, place them on a paper towel to absorb excess oil. Serve hot.

Potatoes and Broccoli

This recipe serves 2. For more, increase ingredients.

½ **bunch broccoli**

2 **potatoes**

Salt and pepper to taste

Milk or parve creamer

1-2 Tbs. margarine

1 Steam or boil broccoli for 15 minutes or until soft. In another pot, at the same time, boil peeled and quartered potatoes.

2 Drain the broccoli and the potatoes.

3 Mash broccoli and potatoes together until very fine and smooth, and season to taste. Add a little milk or parve creamer and 1-2 Tbs. margarine.

Mix well and serve hot.

 ## Potatoes and Spinach

The recipe above can also be made with spinach.

1 Clean the fresh spinach very well, since it is usually very sandy. Wash at least three times, or until the sand is washed out.

2 Tear into small pieces, and steam or boil spinach until soft. Drain.

3 Boil 2 peeled potatoes and drain them.

4 Chop spinach very fine and then add the potatoes, mashing them together. Add a little milk or parve creamer and some margarine. Mix until smooth. Season to taste.

Baked Sweet Potatoes

1 Wash and dry as many sweet potatoes as you need. Pierce them with a fork in a few places to keep them from bursting.

2 Put them on oven rack and bake at 400°F for 50-60 minutes, or until soft.

Hints & Tips

Some potatoes take a longer time to get really soft; therefore, buy the thin, long sweet potatoes. They take only 1 hour to bake. Big ones take 1½ hours or more.

Mashed Sweet Potatoes

1 Wash, dry, pierce, and bake as for *Baked Sweet Potatoes*.

2 After the potatoes are finished baking (about 50-60 minutes), cut in half and scoop out the pulp. Mash.

3 Add a little honey or 1 tsp. of brown sugar, a pat of butter or margarine, and mix well.

4 Spoon into a greased casserole dish and heat in the oven for 10-15 minutes. Serve hot.

Sweet Potato Soufflé

This makes a very good side dish.

1 Wash, pierce, and bake sweet potatoes until soft (about 1 hour or more in a conventional oven).

2 Scoop out pulp and mash.

3 Separate eggs (see page 36). Add margarine, cinnamon, lemon rind, egg yolk, and crushed pineapple to pulp. Mix well. Set aside.

4 Beat egg white until peaks form, and fold gently into mixture.

5 Grease a baking dish, pour in mixture, and dot with a few pieces of margarine on top.

6 Bake at 350°F, until brown on top, about 20-30 minutes. Serve immediately.

2 large sweet potatoes

1 Tbs. margarine,
or butter for dairy

¼ tsp. cinnamon

¼ tsp. grated lemon rind

1 egg

½ cup canned crushed
pineapple, drained

My Mother's (the Best) Potatonik

In the different countries of Eastern Europe, where most of Europe's Jews lived before the Second World War, each area had its own specialties in foods. My mother came from a part of Poland that bordered Rumania, and my father came from Rumania itself, a few hours away. One of their specialties was what was called there *bardebutchenik*. In America, this first cousin of the potato kugel is called *potatonik*.

My dear mother was an expert in making the best potatonik. It was crispy, crunchy, fluffy, and very tasty. When we children (my brother, my sister, and I) were young, my mother made potatonik every Friday for Shabbos. When we woke up early in the morning, the delicious aroma was all over the house and we could not wait to get our teeth into a piece of that potatonik. Once you develop a taste for it, you become addicted to it! When cigarettes were popular, they had a commercial on the radio: "I'd walk a mile for a Camel." In our family, we would walk ten miles for a piece of my mother's potatonik!

As the years went by, my mother baked it only once in a while as a special treat, and as she grew older, it became too hard for her and she stopped baking it altogether. Unfortunately, nobody thought of asking her for the recipe.

When I visited Israel for the first time, around 1965, I took a walk on Ben Yehuda Street in Tel Aviv. As I looked into a dairy restaurant, there, staring at me, was a small potatonik, just like my mother's, only about a quarter of the size that she used to make! Nothing could stop me from going into that restaurant and ordering a piece. I ate some there and took the rest to my hotel room. All that day, I ate nothing but that potatonik. Every time I came to Tel Aviv, which was quite often then, my first stop was that restaurant, until the owner retired and the place was closed.

I asked all of my relatives how to make potatonik. They gave us their recipes, but when we tried to bake it, it was always a disaster and ended up in the garbage can.

After that, I had no potatonik for a number of years, until one day, my brother Leo said to me, "Seymour, how would you like to have a piece of potatonik like Mother used to make?" I thought he would give me the type sold in New York bakeries for Shabbos — a very poor relative of my mother's potatonik — soft, soggy, dry, and tasteless. What he gave me instead was a small, round, crispy, crunchy, fluffy, golden brown and tasty potatonik, just as good as Mother's, in miniature size. My taste buds had a holiday that day. I took the recipe from my sister-in-law, and I have baked it myself many times since then.

Here then is our "secret" recipe for wonderful potatonik, from my sister-in-law, Ruda.

Note: Before starting on this recipe, be sure you have young or fresh Idaho, Russet, or white potatoes. Older potatoes will not give you the same results.

1 Peel potatoes and put them into a large bowl, half-filled with cold water to prevent them from discoloring. Dry them and grate them by hand or with a food processor (I do it by hand) into a large wooden bowl or any other dish. Don't squeeze the water out. (If there's too much water in the bowl, take 2-3 Tbs. out, but leave most of the water in the mixture.)

6-7 large Idaho, Russet, or white potatoes

1 oz. fresh yeast

2½ cups flour

2 eggs

10-4½" round or 4" square by 1½" deep foil baking pans

1 medium onion

2 tsp. salt, or to taste

Dash of pepper (optional)

½ - ¾ tsp. vegetable oil for each foil pan

2 Squeeze and crumble the yeast by hand into the grated potatoes until it's totally absorbed. Then sprinkle about ½ a cup of flour all over the top of the potato mixture. Cover it. I use a plastic sheet, such as a clean plastic bag cut open, first, and then a heavy towel, to keep the towel from getting soiled.

3 Put the bowl in a warm place in the kitchen, on a counter, but *not* in or on the oven. Let the mixture rest for 1 hour or until it rises about ¼ of its size.

4 Meanwhile, let the eggs come to room temperature, and beat slightly. Place the foil baking pans on the counter. The onion may either be chopped and placed in each oiled pan *(see below)* or grated and added to the potato mixture, or both.

5 After the hour is up, if the mixture did not rise enough, wait another 15 minutes or so. Mix the flour that is on top into the mixture. Add the salt, pepper, if using, the eggs, and mix well.

6 Now add the remaining 2 cups of flour, ½ a cup at a time, mixing after each addition. The mixture should be thick but still flowing.

7 Pour ½ - ¾ tsp. of oil into each pan and spread all around with your hands. Then place 1-1½ tsp. of the chopped onions into each pan and spoon 1-1½ large serving spoons of the mixture into each, to fill a little over ¾ of the pan.

8 Preheat oven to 400°F, while letting mixture rest another 20 minutes.

9 Put the pans next to one another in the hot oven and bake for 40 minutes to 1 hour, or longer, until all tops are nice and golden brown. (Since some ovens heat unevenly, some potatoniks may be ready before others. Check them every few minutes after the 40-minute point and move them around as necessary. Take the finished ones out first and leave the pale ones a few minutes longer in the oven, until they are golden brown, too.) Some of the onions may darken in the baking, almost to black, but are still fine to eat.

10 Take the last of the potatoniks out of the oven and let them cool for 10-15 minutes. Carefully remove them from the pans with a rubber or wooden spatula. (Try to avoid piercing the foil pans as they can be reused a few times. Clean them lightly with a metal pad.) Keep the potatoniks on a plate on the counter, *not* in a plastic bag, to keep them crisp until serving.

To serve, cut a potatonik in half through the middle and spread a little butter or margarine on it, adding salt, if needed. Cover with the other half, and you are ready to enjoy the best potatonik in the world!

To freeze potatoniks for up to three weeks: When completely cooled, place them in a plastic bag, and close the bag tightly. To defrost, place potatoniks into the oven at 350°-400°F for 20-25 minutes. They will regain their crispness and taste freshly baked. Keep in an open dish on your counter to retain crispness.

Hints & Tips

OTHER VEGETABLE DISHES

♦ ♦ ♦ ♦ ♦ ♦ ♦ ♦ ♦

Guacamole (Avocado Salad)

1 small onion

1 tomato

2 ripe avocados

½ tsp. lemon juice

2 tsp. chili powder

1 tsp. salt

2 Tbs. vinegar

1 Peel tomato. Chop the onion and the tomato very fine.

2 Mash the avocados with a wooden spoon and add to the onion-tomato mixture. Sprinkle lemon juice over the mixture to keep avocado from turning dark.

3 Add the chili powder, salt, and vinegar. Mix until well blended.

Serve individual portions on lettuce leaves, or with a bowl of crackers or potato chips, or as a cocktail dip for raw vegetables.

Broccoli Kugel or Soufflé

Makes 6-8 portions.

1 Preheat oven to 350°F.

2 Defrost frozen broccoli in one cup of water in a pot over a low flame. Drain. Alternatively, simply leave broccoli at room temperature for one hour and drain well. If using fresh broccoli, cook in small amount of water for 15 minutes or until soft.

3 Chop broccoli into very small pieces.

4 Separate eggs (see page 36). Add to broccoli egg yolks, onion soup mix, mayonnaise, wheat germ, and creamer. Mix well.

5 In another bowl, beat egg whites with an electric mixer or with a whisk or fork until stiff peaks form. Fold into broccoli mixture.

6 Grease a baking pan (about 10" x 7") with margarine or solid shortening. Pour mixture into pan and bake in preheated oven for 45 minutes, until light brown around edges and toward center.

7 Remove from oven, cool 10 minutes, and cut into squares.

Can be cut into slices, wrapped, and frozen. Portions can then be reheated in 350° oven for 15 minutes. Serve hot. Very delicious and healthy.

For a smaller soufflé, use same directions as above, but cut amounts of the ingredients in half. Bake in an 8" round x 2" deep baking dish for about 40 minutes.

2 pkgs. frozen chopped broccoli, or 1½ large bunches fresh broccoli

3-4 eggs

⅓ - ½ envelope onion soup mix, to taste

4 Tbs. mayonnaise

4 Tbs. wheat germ or fine bread crumbs

⅓ - ½ cup parve creamer, or regular sweet cream for dairy

Candied Carrots

5-6 carrots

1 tsp. flour

1-2 Tbs. honey

1 tsp. sugar

1½ Tbs. vegetable oil

⅛ tsp. cinnamon or ginger

1 tsp. lemon rind
(optional)

1 Peel, trim, and slice carrots. Boil for 10 minutes in a pot with barely enough water to cover the carrots.

2 Add remaining ingredients, mix, and let simmer until all liquid is cooked out (about 10-15 minutes longer), stirring occasionally. Keep a close watch to avoid burning. Add more water if needed.

Carrot Delight

¼ cup white raisins

6 carrots

4 Tbs. margarine

2½ Tbs. honey

1 Tbs. lemon juice

¼ tsp. cinnamon

1 Soak raisins in water for 10 minutes.

2 Slice carrots and cook in a little boiling water (about ½") for about 10 minutes.

3 Place carrots into a small oven-safe glass baking dish (1-quart size). Mix with raisins, margarine, honey, lemon juice, and cinnamon.

4 Bake at 375°F, uncovered, for 20-30 minutes. Serve hot.

Carrot Tzimmes

This makes a festive side dish for Shabbos.

1 Peel and slice carrots. Place in enough water to cover ¾ of the carrots. Simmer 10 minutes over a low flame. Add a little more water, if needed.

2 Add all other ingredients. Mix well and let boil for 5 minutes.

3 Continue to boil down to very little water, about 5 minutes more, watching that it doesn't burn, until carrots and apricots are soft. Adjust sweetening (honey, sugar, cinnamon, and lemon peel) to taste.

5-6 medium carrots

1-2 Tbs. honey

1-2 tsp. sugar

2 Tbs. vegetable oil

½ tsp. cinnamon

Peel of half a lemon
(optional)

8-10 dried apricots

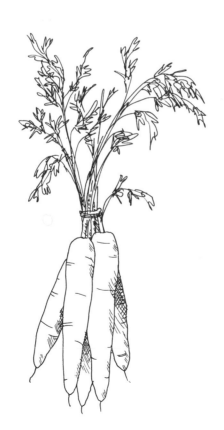

Cauliflower Croquettes

A delicious way to eat your vegetables!

1 head of cauliflower

1 large onion

1-1½ tsp. salt, or to taste

Pepper to taste

½ - ¾ cup matzah meal
or bread crumbs

1-2 eggs
depending on size of cauliflower

2½-3 Tbs. oil or more

1 Cut cauliflower into florets, clean, and either steam or boil for 12-14 minutes, checking every few minutes. (Florets should be thoroughly cooked, but still firm, not soggy.) Set aside to cool for 10 minutes.

2 Meanwhile, chop onion into medium pieces, and sauté until golden. (Optional: Drain on paper towel.)

3 Chop cauliflower into very fine pieces, then use a potato masher to make it smooth. Add fried onions, salt and pepper, matzah meal or bread crumbs, and eggs. Mix well, until very smooth.

4 Put into a dish and refrigerate for 4 hours or overnight.When ready to cook, remove mixture from refrigerator and mix again.

5 Heat a 10" frying pan. Add about 2 Tbs. of oil. Reduce flame to medium-low. When forming croquettes, wet your hands or use rubber gloves. Take large spoonfuls of the mixture, roll between your hands into balls about 2½" in diameter. Flatten on hands to about ½" thick, and put into the frying pan. Frying 3-4 at a time, brown on one side, turn, and fry the other side until light brown. Place on a paper towel to absorb oil. This requires a lot of oil; keep adding ½-1 Tbs. oil when frying pan looks dry, or the croquettes will burn.

Leftover croquettes can make a very good sandwich, hot or cold, between 2 slices of bread or a roll.

Eggplant Salad (Babaganoush)

Serve this as a delicious side dish or appetizer.

1 Preheat oven to 350°F.

2 Cut off the top and peel the eggplant with a vegetable peeler. Cut it lengthwise into ¾" strips.

3 Place into a large dish and salt all over with at least 3 Tbs. kosher salt. Let stand about 20-30 minutes.

4 Wash off all the salt, dry with a paper towel, and place eggplant strips on a baking sheet. Bake at 350°F for about 15 minutes. Let cool off and cut into smaller pieces.

5 Chop onion into large pieces and sauté in about 2 Tbs. oil until golden, not brown.

6 Cut tomato into small chunks. Clean bell pepper inside and cut into ¼" strips, and then cut across into medium-size pieces. Squeeze garlic in garlic press. Place tomatoes, peppers, and garlic with pulp into a large frying pan along with the onions, and sauté on a low flame, adding more oil if needed, for about 10-20 minutes, or until vegetables are soft. Stir every few minutes, and add a few tsp. of water, if too dry.

7 Add eggplant to vegetable mixture. Add salt and pepper to taste. Let cool, then transfer to a covered jar. Refrigerate for a few hours or overnight.

This dish can be eaten warm or cold, as a side dish with meat or fish, or as an appetizer. I prefer it cold, spread on crackers or matzah.

1 large eggplant

3 Tbs. kosher coarse salt

1 large onion

2 Tbs. vegetable oil
and more as needed

1 large tomato

1 red or green bell pepper
(red is sweeter)

2-3 cloves of garlic

¾ tsp. salt, or to taste

Pinch or 2 of pepper,
to taste

Eggplant Salad (Babaganoush) 2

1 medium eggplant

1 tomato

1 onion

½ green or red pepper

1-2 tsp. lemon juice

1 tsp. oil

1 tsp. salt

1-2 tsp. sugar

1 hard-boiled egg
(optional)

1 Preheat oven to 350°F.

2 Wash and dry eggplant. Prick with a fork in a few places and place on a baking sheet. Bake for 45 minutes or until soft.

3 De-seed pepper and bake in oven until soft, about 25 minutes.

4 Meanwhile, chop onion and sauté in oil.

5 Scoop out the baked eggplant and chop with other ingredients. Mix well. Serve cold.

Store leftovers in a closed glass jar in the refrigerator. Pour off any liquid that develops during storage.

Spinach Kugel

8 oz. medium noodles

⅓ cup margarine

2 eggs

2-3 Tbs. onion soup mix, or to taste

½ of a 10-oz. pkg. frozen spinach

⅓ - ½ cup parve non-dairy creamer

Paprika, to taste

Something different but easy to make.

1 Preheat oven to 350°F.

2 Cook noodles according to package directions. Drain well. Soften margarine, and mix together.

3 Thaw and drain the spinach well.

4 Beat eggs and add to noodles. Add onion soup mix and spinach, and then pour in creamer. Mix it all together well.

5 Grease an 8" square baking dish and pour the mixture in. Dot with some margarine, and dust with paprika. Bake for about one hour.

String Beans, Plain

1 Cut ends off string beans and discard. Wash beans well.

2 Bring to a boil 2-3 cups of salted water. Add beans and cook for 15-18 minutes. Drain, and rinse them in cold water.

3 Add margarine, salt, and pepper, or sauté them for a few minutes in some margarine and add salt and pepper. Adjust seasonings to taste; serve immediately.

½ lb. string beans

2 Tbs. margarine
or butter

Salt and pepper, to taste

String Beans and Mushrooms

1 Cut ends off string beans and discard. Wash thoroughly. Cut into 2" lengths. Cook fresh beans for 12-15 minutes in just enough water to cover. (Frozen beans need less cooking time.) Then rinse in cold water.

2 While beans are cooking, clean mushrooms (if fresh are used): Cut off caps, and wash and cut each in half. If using canned, buy the caps only and cut them in half. Season with salt and pepper, and garlic if desired.

3 Chop onion and sauté in margarine until golden. Add mushrooms and sauté together 10 minutes. Drain beans, add to onion and mushrooms, and sauté for a few minutes more. Serve hot.

½ lb. fresh *or* frozen
string beans

4 oz. fresh or canned
mushrooms
use caps only

Salt and pepper to taste

Garlic powder to taste
(optional)

1 small onion

2 Tbs. margarine

Zucchini and Potatoes

1 zucchini

2 potatoes

2 Tbs. margarine
or butter

3-4 Tbs. parve creamer

½ cup tomato sauce

1 Slice zucchini into ¼" slices. Boil zucchini in salted water until soft (about 6-8 minutes).

2 Peel and quarter potatoes and boil in a separate pot.

3 When both are ready, drain. Mash potatoes with a little margarine or butter, and milk or parve creamer. Place potatoes in center of each plate, with boiled zucchini around the potatoes.

4 Heat tomato sauce, pour over both potatoes and zucchini. Serve hot. Makes 2 servings.

Zucchini and Vegetables (Ratatouille)

1 baby eggplant
(optional)

1-2 zucchini

1 onion

1 4-oz. can sliced
mushrooms

Oil, for sautéing

1 medium tomato

½ red pepper

Salt, pepper, and garlic
powder (to taste)

1 Peel and slice eggplant, if using, and cut into small pieces. Trim and discard ends of zucchini. Cut into ¼" slices. Slice, then quarter, tomato. Cut pepper into small pieces.

2 Chop onion and sauté with mushrooms in oil. Add zucchini. Add more oil. Keep stirring for 2-3 minutes.

3 Add tomato pieces, red pepper, and seasonings and simmer, covered, for 8-10 minutes more or until soft. Stir every few minutes, to keep mixture from sticking to pan. Serve hot.

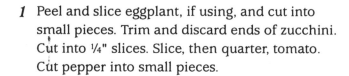

Appetizers

A P P E T I Z E R S

*By definition, an appetizer is a small bit of tasty food
served at the beginning of the meal
to stimulate the appetite.
It can be as simple as a cold wedge of melon
or half a grapefruit, or as fancy as veal sweetbreads.*

♦　♦　♦　♦　♦　♦　♦　♦　♦

In addition to the appetizers listed in this chapter, you can also find suggestions for appetizers in other chapters. For example, *Gefilte Fish*, *Carp and Whitefish,* and *Baked Carp* appear in the *Fish* chapter while *Fresh Fruit Salad* and *Fresh Melon Salad* can be found in the chapter on *Salads*. Be creative — almost any recipe can be prepared and served as an appetizer.

Liver

Although organ meats contain a lot of cholesterol, they are very rich in iron and vitamins. For people who don't have to worry about their cholesterol intake, liver is a very enjoyable appetizer. It is delicious served with a sauce, or chopped with eggs and onions. It's also good just plain broiled as a main course.

Please note that, according to Jewish law, all liver must first be kashered before you cook it. See *Appendix A* for instructions.

After kashering the liver, place it in a greased frying pan over a low flame for about 4 minutes on each side, for medium-well-done. For well-done, cook a minute or two longer on each side. It only takes a few minutes to cook liver, since the kashering process already precooks it. Beef liver is tough and takes longer to cook than other liver. I person-

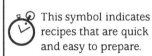 This symbol indicates recipes that are quick and easy to prepare.

ally prefer veal or calf liver, which I like best as liver steak or even as chopped liver. Liver steak is quite good as a main entree, with fried onions on top (see below), or cut into 1½" pieces and simmered in a sauce for 10 minutes and served as an appetizer (see chapter on *Sauces*).

Chicken livers are also very tasty and take just a few minutes to cook in the same way as veal or calf liver. As an appetizer, they are especially delicious with a sauce (see recipe). Just let the chicken livers simmer in the sauce for 10 minutes, and serve hot with fresh challah or a roll.

Fried Onion Rings and Liver

Use any of the milder sweet onions, like Vidalia, Bermuda, white, or Spanish onions.

2 medium onions

4-5 Tbs. oil for sautéing

Cooked liver steaks

1 Peel 2 medium-size onions, then slice thinly into rings.

2 Fry the rings in a good amount of olive or vegetable oil (about 4-5 Tbs.). Do not burn the onions — that would give them a bitter taste. Sauté until golden, then drain on a paper towel. Place onions on the liver steaks and serve.

Onions fried in this manner are also good spooned over mashed potatoes.

Best Chopped Liver

½ lb. chicken livers
(kashered; see Appendix A)

½ lb. calf liver
(kashered; see Appendix A)

1-2 eggs

1-2 onions

1-2 tsp. vegetable oil
or more as needed

Salt to taste

For a special treat.

1 Cook eggs until hard-boiled (see page 260), peel, and let cool off.

2 If you have a meat grinder, grind half the livers, then the eggs, then the rest of the livers.

3 Chop onions and sauté until golden brown. Mix well with liver, add vegetable oil, then chop well until mixture is very smooth. *If still dry, add more vegetable oil.* Season to taste.

If you don't have a meat grinder, chop livers, onions, and eggs in a wooden chopping bowl until very fine and smooth. Then add vegetable oil and mix very thoroughly. Season to taste.

Serve each portion on a bed of lettuce with a few wedges of tomatoes and a few slices of cucumbers on each plate.

 # Chopped Eggs

2-3 eggs

1 medium onion

Oil or mayonnaise
(optional)

Salt and pepper to taste

Simple and quick.

1 Cook eggs until hard-boiled (see page 260), peel, and let cool off.

2 Chop onion and the hard-boiled eggs until the mixture is as smooth as you like it. You can add a little oil or mayonnaise to make it smoother. Add some salt and/or pepper, to taste.

3 To serve, place each portion on a bed of lettuce with sliced tomatoes on each side.

Sweet and Sour Meatballs

A good appetizer for guests.

¾-1½ lbs. ground meat

⅓-½ onion

**½ tsp. garlic powder
or 1 clove of garlic**

1 egg

⅓-½ cup matzah meal

1 tsp. salt, or to taste

Dash of pepper, to taste

**5 Tbs. flour mixed with
½ tsp. paprika**

Oil

1 Chop onion, and mince garlic (if using fresh). Beat the egg.

2 Mix ground meat with onion, garlic, beaten egg, matzah meal, and seasonings.

3 Form meatballs by taking spoonfuls of ground meat mixture, and rolling them between wetted hands until smooth and round, about the size of walnuts.

4 Pour flour and paprika into a paper or plastic bag. Place four meatballs in the bag at a time; shake to coat.

5 Brown the meatballs in 2 Tbs. of oil, adding more oil when needed. Then place them on a paper towel to absorb excess oil. When all the meatballs have been browned, begin preparing the sauce.

Sauce:

6 Chop and sauté onion.

1½-2 cups water

1 small to medium onion

1½-2 tsp. sugar

1-2 tsp. flour mixture
(left over from above)

Salt and pepper to taste

**Small pinch of sour salt
or 1-2 tsp. lemon juice**

7 Boil water in a 3-quart pot. Add to the boiling water the onion, sugar, flour, seasonings, and sour salt or lemon juice. Mix well, adjusting seasonings to taste, and then add the meatballs.

8 Simmer for 20-30 minutes; stir occasionally so onions don't stick to bottom of pot. Adjust taste.

The same recipe can be used for larger meat patties, up to about 2½" long by 1½" thick, sometimes served as an entree.

Sweetbreads

¾ lb. veal sweetbreads

Salt and pepper to taste

1 large onion

2 cups water

1 tsp. sugar

¾ of a can
sliced mushrooms

2 Tbs. matzah meal
or very fine bread crumbs

Sweetbreads are organ meats, like liver, and therefore contain a lot of cholesterol. That is why I cook this delicious dish only about three times a year, for special occasions.

Beef sweetbreads take more than two hours to cook. I prefer using veal sweetbreads which are leaner and take only half an hour to cook.

1 Clean sweetbreads by cutting away all skin, fat, and membranes. Cut into bite-size pieces. Season with salt and pepper.

2 Cut mushrooms into halves.

3 Chop and sauté onion.

4 In a pot, bring the water to a boil and add salt, pepper, sugar, sweetbreads, mushrooms, and sautéed onions. Let simmer 15 minutes.

5 Add matzah meal or bread crumbs and mix well, stirring every few minutes to prevent onions from sticking to the bottom of the pot. Simmer for another 15 minutes.

Check to see if meat is soft and taste is the way you want it. Sauce should be slightly thick, not watery. If needed, add some more bread crumbs and spices.

Chicken Fricassee

This recipe takes a little longer than others to cook, but if you will take the time (about two to three hours), you'll say, "It was worth the time spent."

This is a delicious dish. You can make enough for two or three meals or more, use what you need right away, and freeze the rest for another time.

I save the chicken parts for this dish from the chickens I use every week, putting them into a plastic bag and freezing them until I have enough to make a meal. Or, you can ask your butcher if he sells these parts separately — some do.

Before you start to cook this dish, please note: The gizzards and necks take about 1½-2½ hours to cook. The wings take 30-60 minutes. If you add chicken livers, these only take 5-10 minutes, but they have to be kashered first. (See *Appendix A: Kashering Liver*.) If you use giblets from broilers or fryers (smaller birds) they take less time to cook than those from pullets. Therefore, store them in a separate bag.

1 Clean chicken parts thoroughly. Remove pinfeathers from wings or singe them over a stove flame. Rinse and pat dry with paper towels. Sprinkle giblets with 1 tsp. of salt, or to taste, and a little pepper.

2 Into a paper or plastic bag put flour, paprika, and garlic powder. Mix well. Add 5-6 pieces of chicken at a time, shaking the bag until they are well coated.

3 Heat 2-3 Tbs. of oil in a frying pan to the sizzling point, add coated chicken pieces, includ-

1½ lbs. or more
chicken parts
*Necks, wings, and giblets
(gizzards and kashered livers)
cut into bite-size pieces*

5 Tbs. flour

½-¾ tsp. paprika

1-2 tsp. garlic powder

Oil for browning
chicken parts

1 medium onion

2½-3 cups water

1-1½ Tbs. sugar,
or to taste

1 tsp. + 1 tsp. (for sauce)
salt, or to taste

Pepper to taste

Small pinch of sour salt
(citric acid)
or 1-2 Tbs. lemon juice

2-3 Tbs. raisins
(optional)

ing the wings, and reduce heat. Brown pieces on one side, and turn and brown the other side. Continue until all pieces are browned. Place giblets on a paper towel to drain the oil.

4 Now take the wings and place them, covered, into the refrigerator. You will need them later, after the necks and gizzards have cooked for at least an hour.

5 Chop onion and fry until golden, stirring in a little of the flour mixture (about 1-3 tsp.).

6 In a separate, larger pot (about 3-quart size), boil the water, add sugar, salt, pepper, and sour salt or lemon juice, a little bit at a time, checking taste each time you add more. Mix well.

When taste is right, add onions and mix again. Add necks and gizzards. Let simmer 1½ hours, covered, but with lid slightly askew, to allow steam to escape. Stir frequently, so that onions do not stick to bottom of pot. Check often to see if more water is needed, adding a little at a time.

Cook giblets until almost soft: 1 hour for fryer giblets, 2 hours for pullet ones (it all depends on the age of the chickens).

7 Then add the wings together with the raisins (if using) to the pot. Bring to a boil, reduce to simmer, and let cook for 30-60 minutes or until soft.

8 Check necks and gizzards for softness. When almost soft, add livers (if using), let simmer for 5-10 more minutes, or until all parts are soft enough to eat. Adjust taste. Do not overcook, or giblets will fall apart. It should have a pleasant sweet and sour taste, and the sauce should be slightly thick.

Alternative:

If you don't want a sweet and sour taste, eliminate sour salt, sugar, and raisins. This will give you a "pot roast" taste. All other ingredients remain the same, as does the cooking time.

Hints & Tips

As an appetizer, Chicken Fricassee goes well with fresh challah, or as a main entree, with mashed potatoes, rice or potato pancakes, carrots, and broccoli.

Soups

SOUPS

A clear, light soup is a good start to a full meal.
A thick, hearty soup can accompany a light meal
or can be filling and satisfying enough to serve
as a meal in itself.

Soups are a welcome part of any meal,
especially in the winter, when a hot cup of soup
warms you up after coming inside from the cold.

♦　♦　♦　♦　♦　♦　♦　♦　♦

The recipes here are for three or four cups of soup, but you can increase the ingredients and make more. All you have to do is add a little water or milk (for a dairy meal only, of course), or any other liquid appropriate for the soup, mix it in, and bring it to a boil. Since soups will stay fresh for a number of days, you can store leftovers in the refrigerator to heat up as needed.

A soup that calls for milk in the recipe can be made suitable for a meat ("fleishig") meal by substituting the same amount of parve coffee creamer for the milk. To make a soup thicker and creamier, mash the vegetables with a potato masher or place all the vegetables into a blender or a food processor and blend them for a few seconds until they are creamy; then add them to the liquid and mix well. Another method is to mix 1-2 tablespoons of flour or cornstarch with cold water (about 3 Tbs.) to form a thick paste. Add this to the cooking soup and let it simmer, stirring occasionally until soup is thickened. You can also add a Tbs. of semolina to a simmering vegetable soup. Choose whichever method appeals to you. Each should give the same result of thickening the soup.

 This symbol indicates recipes that are quick and easy to prepare.

When it comes to making chicken soup, I find it advisable to cool the soup to room temperature after it is cooked, and remove the chicken and all the soup greens. Cover the soup and let it chill in the refrigerator for a few hours or overnight. You will find that all the chicken fat has solidified at the top, so you can remove it in "sheets." Even though the soup will lose a little of its *ta'am* (taste) this way, it will be 100% healthier without all that fat.

You can also find dried soup mixes at your kosher butcher or grocery store that only require you to add water and simmer for ¾ hour. They come in several different varieties, and you can improve on their flavor by adding fresh, sliced vegetables according to your taste. Let it all simmer according to package directions and you have a delicious soup. To make a hearty soup to accompany a meat meal, add chicken giblets or pieces of meat in addition to lots of fresh vegetables.

A number of recipes call for chicken broth cubes. Please note that these cubes come in parve or meat versions. Look carefully at the package before using, when adding to a parve soup that will be served with a parve or dairy meal.

Best Fresh Vegetable Soup

3-4 oz. large dried
lima beans

5-6 cups water

2 tsp. salt

Dash of pepper

1½-2 carrots

1½ stalks celery

1 medium onion

1 parsnip

½ cup medium barley

1 large potato

½ small can of sweet peas,
or ½ package frozen

1 Wash the lima beans and soak them overnight in water. This will save an hour of cooking time the next day.

2 Slice carrots and celery, chop onion, and cut parsnip and potato into 1" bite-size pieces.

3 Bring water to a boil. Add salt and pepper, to taste. When water boils, add the drained beans and all other ingredients except peas. Bring to a boil again; reduce flame.

4 Simmer for 20 minutes, and then add peas. Simmer 15 minutes more or until all vegetables and lima beans are soft. If canned sweet peas are used, add them for the last 5 minutes of cooking.

Quick Vegetable Soup

2 cups water

2 cups warm milk,
or parve coffee whitener

2 tsp. salt,
or 2 bouillon cubes

Pepper, to taste

½ lb. frozen mixed
vegetables

1 tomato
or 3-4 Tbs. tomato paste

1 onion

2 Tbs. butter or margarine

3 Tbs. flour

1 Pour water and milk, or substitute, into a large pot. Add salt (or bouillon cubes) and pepper, then add mixed vegetables and tomato, cut in small pieces, or tomato paste.

2 Separately, chop onion into medium-size pieces and sauté in melted butter or margarine, until golden. Stir in flour, and lower flame. Sauté 2 more minutes. Add to milk, water, and vegetables.

3 Simmer until all ingredients are soft, about 20 minutes. Adjust seasonings and add more water or milk, if needed.

Quick Tomato Soup

1 Pour tomato juice into a medium-size pot. Heat to boiling, lower flame, and simmer.

2 Chop celery and onion, and mince garlic. Add celery, onion, garlic, and seasonings to tomato juice. Cook until vegetables are soft, about 15-20 minutes.

2-3 cups tomato juice

1 stalk celery

1 small onion

1 clove garlic

Salt and pepper, to taste

Bean Soup

This will make 5 servings or more.

1 The night before cooking the soup, wash beans and discard any that are bad or moldy. Place in a glass jar and fill with tap water to about 3" over top of beans. Close lid tightly.

2 In the morning, discard water and pour 6 cups of fresh water into a pot. Add soaked beans.

3 Chop the onion and mince the garlic. Add to pot. Season with salt and pepper to taste. Add bay leaf.

4 Simmer 20 minutes. Add egg flakes, bring to boil, and simmer another 15 minutes or until beans are soft. Discard bay leaf.

Adjust taste, adding salt and pepper if needed.

⅓ package dried lima beans

½ package dried kidney beans

6 cups water

1-2 chicken broth cubes (optional)

1 small bay leaf

1 clove garlic

Salt and pepper, to taste

1 medium onion

4 oz. (½ package) egg flakes (farfel)

Borscht (Like My Mother Made It)

1 bunch beets
*about 1¼-1¾ lb. per bunch,
or 3-4 beets, depending on size*

Fresh garlic, to taste

6 cups water

Dash of pepper

½-1 tsp. sugar

2 eggs

This is the best tasting borscht I've ever had.

1 Peel, trim, and cut beets into small pieces or slices. Add salt and fresh garlic to taste.

2 Boil in the 6 cups of water for at least 45 minutes (longer for older beets: up to 1½ hours), adding more water if needed. Add pepper and sugar to taste. Let cool off.

Alternatively, you can use ready-made borscht and continue as below.

Separate liquid from cooked beets. *Use beets as a side dish.*

3 Add two slightly beaten eggs to the beet liquid. Using two medium-size pots, pour mixture back and forth between the two pots, about 8-10 times, or mix in a blender for 10-15 seconds.

Serve cold with a hot potato.

Cream of Potato Soup

1   Cut potatoes into small pieces, chop onion, and slice celery stalk. Boil potatoes, onion, celery and garlic *(optional)* in water, or milk/water combination, for 10-12 minutes, until tender. Stir in margarine or butter.

2   Mash with a potato masher or put all into blender and blend for 10-15 seconds, until smooth. Season with salt and pepper to taste. Serve hot.

To thicken, add 2 tablespoons of fine bread crumb mix into soup. Serve hot.

If you use garlic, peel and put into water while cooking; discard after cooking, or put into blender with other vegetables.

1-2 medium potatoes

1 medium onion

1 stalk celery

1 small clove garlic
(optional)

1 Tbs. margarine,
or butter for dairy use

4 cups water
or 2 cups each of water
and milk (for dairy use)

½ tsp. salt, or to taste

Dash of pepper

2 Tbs. fine bread crumbs

Cream of Mushroom Soup (Dairy)

1   Clean mushrooms if using fresh ones. Chop fine and brown lightly in butter or margarine.

2   Blend in flour, pour in milk gradually, and cook in top part of a double boiler for 20 minutes, stirring frequently. Season to taste.

6 oz. fresh or 4 oz.
canned mushrooms

4 Tbs. butter or margarine

3½ Tbs. flour

5 cups milk

1-2 tsp. salt

Dash or two of pepper,
to taste

Cream of Celery Soup (Dairy)

2 cups diced celery

1 small onion

1½ cups boiling water

3 Tbs. butter or margarine

4 Tbs. flour

3 cups milk

1½ tsp. salt

⅛ tsp. pepper

1 Grate onion. Cook the diced celery and onions in water for 10-12 minutes and set aside.

2 Melt butter or margarine, blend in flour, add milk, and cook, stirring constantly until thick.

Combine with cooked celery, onions and liquid. Season as indicated or to taste.

Add more water and/or milk if soup is too thick.

 ## Cream of Tomato Soup (Dairy)

1 8-oz. can tomato sauce

¼ medium onion

1½ Tbs. butter or margarine

1 Tbs. flour

2 cups milk

½ tsp. salt

Dash of pepper

1 In a medium-size pot, bring tomato sauce to a boil. Dice onion, and add to pot. Bring to boil again, remove from heat, and set aside.

2 In a separate small pot, melt butter and blend in flour. Add to tomato sauce. Add milk, salt, and pepper. Bring to boil, stirring constantly for 3 minutes. If too thick, add ¼ to ½ cup water. Adjust seasonings to taste.

Split Pea Soup

1 Wash peas and place into a pot or glass jar. Pour enough cold water into the pot to cover the peas, plus 2-3" more. Let the peas soak for 5 hours or overnight. Drain before using.

2 Mince garlic, and boil in water with salt and pepper. Dice carrot and chop onions, and add with peas to water. Bring it all to a boil again and simmer for 15 minutes.

3 Add frankfurter slices, if using, and let simmer until peas are soft, another 15 minutes. Adjust seasoning.

1 cup dried split peas

4 cups water

Salt and pepper, to taste

1 clove garlic

1 carrot

1 small onion

1-2 frankfurters, cut into ½" slices
(optional)

 ## Quick Peas and Egg Flakes Soup

1 Cook egg flakes according to directions on the package. Drain in a colander or strainer, let warm water run over egg flakes, and set aside.

2 In another pot, bring water to boil. Add broth cubes, cooked egg flakes, and sweet peas. Simmer till peas are soft. (Canned peas are already very soft, and will need only warming.) Season to taste.

3 If too watery, mix 1-1½ Tbs. flour into ¼ cup cold water. Stir to remove lumps and add to soup. Mix well. Or, stir in ½ Tbs. cornstarch dissolved in cold water. Let soup simmer 3-5 minutes.

4 oz. (½ package) egg flakes (farfel)

4-5 cups water

1-2 chicken broth cubes

1 10-oz. pkg. frozen sweet peas or ½-1 15-oz. can of the best small sweet peas

Salt and pepper, to taste

Chicken Soup

A tradition for Shabbos and Holiday meals.

2½ quarts cold water

2 tsp. salt

1-2 consomme cubes
(optional — gives a good taste)

4 oz. large lima beans,
washed
(do not soak overnight)

1 3½ lb. pullet in quarters

2 cloves garlic

Soup Vegetables:

1-2 carrots

1 white turnip

1 parsnip

1 onion

1 stalk celery

½ bunch parsley

½ bunch dill

1 leek

1 Pour 2-2½ quarts water (8-10 cups) into a large pot. Add salt and consomme cubes (optional). Add lima beans, chicken that has been cleaned with all fat removed, and the 2 peeled, whole cloves of garlic, with a slit in each clove. Bring to boil, reduce to simmer, and cover pot, leaving the lid partway off the pot to let steam escape. Let simmer for 30 minutes. Skim foam from top.

2 In the meantime, peel carrots, turnip, parsnip, and onion, slice them into desired size, and add to soup. Clean all other soup vegetables (cut off dark green ends of leek and discard) and add them to the soup. Let simmer for one more hour.

Check the seasoning, adjusting to your taste. Test chicken to see if it's soft and ready. If not, let cook another 15 minutes (not longer, or chicken will fall apart).

3 Remove chicken with a large perforated spoon and place it on a large plate. If you do not want the vegetables to be served in the soup, remove and discard them, reserving whichever ones you do choose to serve, such as carrots and parsnip. Save the lima beans for a side dish or to eat with the soup.

4 Cool the soup. Place the pot of soup in the refrigerator. After a few hours, the chicken fat will be solidified at the top of the soup. Remove this fat before reheating.

Serve hot soup with noodles, egg flakes, rice, or matzah balls. Refrigerated leftovers are good for 2-4 days.

Chicken Soup with Brisket or Flanken

Chicken and beef, when cooked together, give the soup an especially good taste.

1 Rinse chicken, lima beans, and brisket or flanken. (Do not soak beans, just wash them.) Pour cold water into a large pot. Add chicken quarters, beef, and lima beans. Bring to a boil, skim foam, and reduce flame to a simmer.

2 Let soup simmer for 30-45 minutes with the pot cover askew, leaving enough of an opening to let the steam escape.

3 In the meantime, clean all the soup vegetables: peel carrot, parsnip, and turnip, and cut them through the middle and then in half. Cut celery into 3-4" lengths. Make sure all the vegetables are cleaned and checked according to guidelines in *Appendix B*. Cut off parsley and dill stems and add greens to the soup. Next, add peeled onion and whole garlic.

Bring soup to a boil again, then reduce flame to simmer. Cook for one more hour and check to see if chicken is soft. Adjust according to your taste, adding salt as needed.

4 Remove chicken, if soft. Beef may need more cooking, perhaps ½ hour or more. Add more water, if needed.

5 After beef is ready, discard soup greens and garlic; reserve carrots and parsnip to serve with soup. Save lima beans to serve as a side dish or with soup.

Noodles, egg flakes, egg barley shapes, or matzah balls may be served with the soup.

1 3½-4 lb. pullet, quartered

4 oz. large dried lima beans

2 lbs. lean brisket or flanken, with fat removed

2½ quarts (10 cups) cold water

Soup Vegetables:

1 carrot

1 parsnip

1 turnip

1 stalk celery

½ bunch parsley

½ bunch dill

1 onion

2 cloves fresh garlic

1½-2 tsp. salt, or to taste

If you like chicken vegetable soup, you can divide the clear soup into two parts. One part can be served as clear chicken broth with noodles.

The other part can be served as vegetable soup. Remove and discard parsley and dill. Remove lima beans, setting them aside. All other vegetables can be squeezed through a strainer. Then add the lima beans. When serving the soup, you can also add some noodle product to give the soup more body.

Barley and Mushroom Soup

½-¾ cup medium barley

4-6 cups water

2-3 oz. canned or fresh sliced mushrooms

2 marrow bones
available from the butcher

Salt and pepper, to taste

¼ cup chopped onions

2 carrots

1 Cook barley according to the directions on the package. Alternatively, rinse and sort barley and let it soak overnight in 4-6 cups of water. Next day, drain the barley in a strainer and refill the pot with fresh water. Bring it to a boil and add the barley.

2 Add mushrooms and marrow bones. Bring to a boil and skim the foam. Add seasonings, onions, and sliced and halved carrots (carrots may be quartered if they are very large).

3 Bring to a boil again, lower flame, and simmer until barley is soft, 45 minutes to 1 hour, adding more water if needed.

Matzah Balls (Kneidlach)

1 Beat eggs lightly with a fork. Add salt and oil.

2 Stir in matzah meal, moistening thoroughly, then slowly add water, a little at a time, until mixture begins to clump.

3 Cover bowl and place in refrigerator for 15-30 minutes. When you are ready to begin cooking, stir mixture again, adding seltzer.

4 Boil 1½-2 quarts of water in a pot with 1 tsp. of salt added. Put a few drops of oil in the palm of one hand and spread all over your palms and fingers. *(This will help keep the dough from sticking to them. Repeat as necessary as you go.)*

5 Form balls about the size of walnuts by rolling bits of dough between your palms. Drop each ball into the pot of boiling water. *(Some people drop them directly into the simmering chicken soup.)*

6 Simmer, covered, on a very low flame for about 20 minutes. You can remove the kneidlach and refrigerate them in a covered dish, or serve immediately, hot. *To reheat, simply add to hot soup just before serving!*

2 eggs

1 tsp. salt

¼ cup olive, walnut, or peanut oil

1 cup matzah meal

½ cup water

¼ cup seltzer

1½-2 quarts water

Main Courses

Chicken Dishes

Turkey Dishes

Duck Dishes

Beef Dishes

Steaks and Chops

Veal Dishes

Ground Meat Dishes

Fish Dishes

CHICKEN
DISHES

◆ ◆ ◆ ◆ ◆ ◆ ◆ ◆ ◆

Orange/Onion Spiced Chicken

1 3½-4 lb. chicken, whole

2 Tbs. orange marmalade

½ cup orange juice

½ cup water

¼ - ½ envelope
onion soup mix

½ tsp. garlic powder

Dash of pepper

½ - 1 tsp. ketchup
(optional)

A different kind of taste.

1 Preheat oven to 350°F. Place chicken into roasting pan.

2 Measure all remaining ingredients into a glass or a jar. Mix very well, so that all ingredients are dissolved into the orange juice. Pour half over the chicken.

3 Cover pan and bake 40 minutes. Uncover. Pour the remaining sauce over the chicken, if needed. Bake, uncovered, another 45 minutes. (Turn chicken over for last 30 minutes of baking.) Baste every 15 minutes.

Adjust seasoning, if necessary.

 This symbol indicates recipes that are quick and easy to prepare.

Chicken in Italian Marinade

Here's an easy and tasty dish!

1 The night before you plan to cook the chicken, rub it with Italian dressing, all over, inside and out. (Make sure the dressing is kosher and parve.) Sprinkle with pepper, salt (if using), and garlic powder. Place in a glass dish, cover with foil, and leave in refrigerator overnight to marinate.

2 The next day, preheat the oven to 350°F. Remove chicken from glass dish, place in roasting pan, and pour over the chicken any juices that may have accumulated. Sprinkle with paprika.

3 Cover pan with foil, place in oven and bake for 45 minutes. Turn chicken over. If too dry, brush with more Italian dressing. Cover chicken with foil and bake another 30-45 minutes.

1 3½-4 lb. chicken
whole or in quarters

**⅓ - ½ cup parve
Italian salad dressing**

1-2 dashes pepper

½-1 tsp. salt
(optional)

1 tsp. garlic powder

½ tsp. paprika

To Brown Any Chicken

After 1 hour of baking, remove cover and bake uncovered for 15-20 minutes. Turn chicken, baste with more dressing or its own juices, and bake another 10-15 minutes.

Hints & Tips

Best Chicken Pot Roast

1 3½-4½ lb. pullet,
quartered

3 Tbs. oil

1 large onion, chopped

1 tsp. salt, or to taste

Pinch of pepper, or to taste

1 tsp. garlic powder

Paprika

1-2 cloves garlic

2-2½ cups water

2-3 potatoes
(optional)

2-3 carrots
(optional)

It has to be the best — it's my mother's!

1 Wash chicken pieces. Remove fat. Dry with paper towels. Mince one piece of fresh garlic and rub into chicken.

2 Heat the oil in a large frying pan. Place the chicken quarters into the oil and brown each side for about 10-15 minutes. Remove quarters from frying pan and put into a Dutch oven or a heavy pot.

3 Chop onion and, in the same oil, fry until golden, adding more oil if needed. *Do not burn onions.* Put into the pot with the four quarters of chicken.

4 Dust chicken with salt, pepper, garlic powder, and paprika. Add 2-2½ cups of boiling water, pouring into pot slowly so that it won't splash. Add fresh garlic, if using. Bring to a boil, reduce heat and simmer on lowest flame. Cover pot slightly askew, and cook for 30 minutes. Check for seasoning; add a little more water, as needed.

5 Peel potatoes and carrots. Cut into quarters and add to chicken pot. Cook for another 45 minutes. Check for taste and adjust seasoning as needed. Add more boiling water if necessary. Check to see if chicken is ready. Do not overcook. Total cooking time is 1½-1¾ hours, not longer.

6 Discard solid pieces of garlic. Remove chicken, potatoes, and carrots from sauce. Cool and refrigerate. Sauce will solidify after a few hours or overnight. You can skim off and discard the chicken fat before re-warming the chicken and vegetables in the sauce. Add water if needed. *If more sauce is needed, see recipes for sauces.*

Roast Chicken

This is everybody's favorite.

1 Preheat oven to 350°F.

2 Clean chicken, rinse, and dry with a paper towel.

3 Squeeze garlic in a garlic press and rub garlic onto the inside of chicken. Add a little pepper to the inside. Do not sprinkle salt on the inside of the cavity. Sprinkle outside of chicken with salt, a little pepper, and garlic powder to taste. Dust chicken with paprika.

4 Wrap tightly with aluminum foil and put into roasting pan. Bake for 45 minutes. Open foil and increase oven temperature to 375°F. Bake chicken for another 10-15 minutes on each side. Baste each side two times. Check to see if chicken is ready.

For crisper chicken, do not wrap in foil. Rub chicken with vegetable oil or Italian dressing all over before seasoning it. Bake open 1-1½ hours on a rack in a roasting pan, basting every 20 minutes.

This recipe is good with mashed potatoes or potato latkes, broccoli, corn on the cob, and a vegetable salad.

1 3-3½ lb. broiler, whole

1 clove garlic

⅛ tsp. pepper

1 tsp. salt, to taste

1 tsp. garlic powder, or to taste

Paprika to dust chicken

Baked Chicken

1 3½-4 lb. chicken
(pullet or broiler),
in quarters

3-4 tsp. parve
Italian dressing

1-1½ Tbs. garlic powder

salt, to taste

⅛-¼ tsp. pepper,
or to taste

½ tsp. paprika,
enough to dust chicken

2-3 potatoes
(optional)

½ cup orange juice
mixed with ¼ cup water

An appetizing dish.

1 The night before baking the chicken, clean it and remove fat. Rub Italian dressing or vegetable oil all over, inside and outside chicken. Combine garlic powder, salt, and pepper, and dust chicken with mixture. Put chicken into a baking dish, cover and refrigerate overnight.

2 The next day, turn the chicken over in the seasoning one hour before baking.

3 Heat oven to 375°F. Discard any liquid that may have accumulated in the baking dish overnight. Remove the chicken and add a little oil to the baking dish. Dust chicken with paprika. Place chicken, skin-side down, in baking dish. Bake uncovered for 30 minutes.

4 Peel and quarter potatoes. Add to chicken.

5 Baste chicken with the orange juice mixture, and then turn skin-side up to bake for 30-45 minutes more, uncovered. Baste chicken and potatoes every 15-20 minutes. Test for doneness and adjust the seasoning.

This recipe is good with kasha or potatoes and broccoli (see recipes) and a fresh vegetable salad.

Chicken with Oregano

Salt-free — but very tasty. The best no-salt seasoning uses herbs instead of salt; mix enough for stock, which you can use anytime. If you are on a restricted salt-free diet, ask your doctor if these herbs are okay for you to use.

6 tsp. garlic powder

3 tsp. oregano

⅓-½ tsp. black pepper

1½ tsp. lemon peel

1 3-lb. broiler,
cut into quarters

1 Preheat oven to 350°F.

2 Place all seasonings into an empty spice container and shake until all the spices are mixed well. *This will make enough herb mixture to spice seven chickens or more.*

3 Clean and wash chicken quarters. Put the chicken skin-side down and dust ½ tsp. of the spice mixture all over the chicken. Turn chicken skin-side up and sprinkle ¼ tsp. of the spice mixture on each quarter. Move skin aside while spicing underneath, then replace skin on chicken.

4 Place chicken in a baking dish, cover with aluminum foil, and refrigerate for 1 hour *(optional)*.

5 Place chicken, uncovered, into oven and bake for 50 minutes, basting every 15-20 minutes with its own juices. If needed, pour ⅓ cup boiling water into sides of pan.

6 Turn chicken skin-side down and let it brown for about 10 to 15 minutes. Turn chicken skin-side up again and bake for another 10 minutes. Baste chicken. The total baking time should be about 1 hour and 15 minutes.

If you like to have a baked potato with your meal, pierce a potato with a fork in a few places and put it into the oven to bake at the same time that you begin baking the chicken.

Hints & Tips

Baked Garlic Chicken

1 3-4 lb. broiler,
in quarters or whole

2 Tbs. margarine

3-4 cloves fresh garlic

Salt and pepper, to taste

Paprika, to dust chicken

⅓ cup boiling water

This one is for garlic lovers.

1 Preheat oven to 350°F. Grease the baking pan with margarine.

2 Clean chicken. Mince garlic and rub it onto all sides of the chicken. Dust with salt, pepper, and paprika.

3 Cover pan and bake for 30 minutes. Then remove cover and add boiling water. Leaving cover off, bake for another 45-60 minutes, turning the chicken once or twice. Baste chicken every 20 minutes.

To test if chicken is ready, prick a thigh with a fork. If the juice that comes out is clear, the chicken is done.

This recipe is good with barley-shape mixture, carrots, string beans, and a fresh vegetable salad (see recipes).

Sweet and Sour Chicken

A very good change.

1 Preheat oven to 350°F.

2 Put chicken pieces skin-side down into a shallow baking dish.

3 Mix dressing, onion soup or sautéed onion, and apricot preserves with a little cold water or orange juice (1 or more Tbs.), just enough to thin out mixture. Pour this mixture over the chicken.

4 Bake uncovered for 40 minutes, turning pieces after 20 minutes. Then bake covered for 20 minutes more, or until soft.

This recipe is good with rice and green vegetables or kasha and broccoli (see recipes for side dishes).

1 2½-3½ lb. broiler, in quarters

¼ 8-oz. bottle dark Russian dressing

¼-⅓ envelope onion soup mix or 1 small onion chopped and sautéed, plus ½ tsp. salt, or to taste

¼-⅓ 8-oz. jar apricot preserves

1 Tbs. water or orange juice

Best Southern "Fried" Baked Chicken

1 3-3½ lb. broiler, cut into eighths, washed and with all the fat removed

1 tsp. salt

⅛ tsp. pepper

½ tsp. garlic powder

½ tsp. paprika

3 cups corn flakes crushed into small crumbs

⅓ cup mayonnaise

Tasty and healthier than regular fried chicken.

1 Preheat oven to 400°F.

2 Sprinkle all the chicken pieces with salt.

3 Put all seasonings and corn flakes crumbs into a plastic bag, mixing well.

4 Take one piece of chicken at a time and coat with mayonnaise, and then put coated chicken into the plastic bag with the seasoned crumbs and shake until all the sides of the chicken are covered. Then place the chicken on a baking sheet that was greased lightly with margarine.

Repeat this method until all chicken pieces have been covered and placed on the baking sheet. Leave some space between each piece.

5 Bake chicken for 40-45 minutes, until golden brown.

This recipe is also good with french fries or mashed potatoes, sweet corn on the cob, and broccoli.

If you want baked potatoes, put a few in the oven at the same time as the chicken to make baked potatoes. (Don't forget to pierce them first.) Serve hot from the oven.

Hints & Tips

Chinese Chicken

You will think you are dining in China.

1 Wash chicken and remove all fat.

2 Cut onions into thin slices, and sauté. Place sautéed onions on the bottom of a large roasting pan which has been lightly greased with margarine. Place all the pieces of chicken on top of the onions, skin-side down.

3 Mix the remaining ingredients well and pour over chicken. Cover the pan and leave in the refrigerator for one hour. Meanwhile, preheat oven to 350°F.

4 Turn the pieces of chicken over (skin-side up) and bake for 20 minutes, covered.

5 Remove cover, turn chicken again, skin-side down. Bake for 20 minutes more. Turn chicken over again, facing skin-side up. Baste chicken, test for taste. If too tart, add 1 tsp. of honey to the sauce, mix, and baste again.

Reduce the heat to 325°F. Continue to bake uncovered until the chicken is ready (about 30 minutes more). Baste a few more times, check taste, adjust seasoning, adding orange juice if needed.

1 3½-4 lb. broiler, cut into eighths

1 onion

5-6 oz. orange or apricot preserves

¼ tsp. ground ginger *(optional)*

¾ tsp. garlic powder

1 Tbs. soy sauce

¼ cup orange juice

1-2 tsp. lemon juice

Paprika to dust chicken (about ½ tsp.)

This recipe is very good with rice or potato pancakes, sweet carrots, asparagus, or Brussels sprouts.

Hints & Tips

Quick Baked Half-Chicken and Potatoes

2 quarters of a small broiler chicken

½ tsp. salt

Pinch of pepper

½ tsp. garlic powder

Paprika

2 potatoes

A quick supper that's really tasty!

This recipe is for when you are in a hurry. It takes only one hour to prepare and bake completely. While the chicken is in the oven, cook a vegetable like broccoli or carrots.

1 Preheat oven to 375°F.

2 Wash chicken, remove all fat, dry with paper towel. Place the chicken in a baking pan, 1½" deep. Season chicken with all the spices.

3 Place pan into oven. Wash the two potatoes, pierce them with a fork, and put them on the oven rack at the same time. Bake for 20 minutes.

4 Add ¼-½ cup boiling water to the chicken, if needed. Turn chicken and baste. Bake for 15 minutes. Turn again and baste. Bake for another 10-15 minutes, or until chicken and potatoes are done.

Glazed Chicken

This has a nice, sweet flavor.

1 Preheat oven to 375°F.

2 Wash chicken and remove as much fat as you can. Mince garlic and rub it on the inside of the chicken.

3 Mix all other ingredients with the orange juice. Coat all sides of chicken with the mixture.

4 Bake for 50-60 minutes, basting every 20 minutes. Add more orange juice if needed.

This goes well with any stuffing recipe, if desired. See recipes for stuffing. Serve with vegetable salad, mashed potatoes mixed with chopped spinach, and sweet carrots.

Here's another glaze you may want to try:

Combine 2 tsp. lemon juice (or a bit more) and 2 tsp. honey (more, if you like things sweeter). Mix well and coat chicken just as it's finished baking. Put it back under the broiler for 1-2 minutes. Take it out, turn the chicken, coat the other side and put it back under the broiler for another 1-2 minutes. *Delicious!*

3 lb. broiler, whole

1 clove of garlic

½ tsp. garlic powder, or to taste

½ tsp. paprika

2 Tbs. soy sauce

2 Tbs. honey

2 Tbs. orange marmalade

⅓ cup orange juice

3 Tbs. orange liqueur
(optional)

Cornish Game Hens

**1-2 Cornish hens,
1½ lbs. each**

½ cup margarine

¼ cup flour

½ cup fine bread crumbs

½-1 tsp. salt, or to taste

⅛ tsp. pepper

½-¾ tsp. paprika

Cornish hens might be small, but they make a great meal for company!

1 Preheat oven to 350°F.

2 Cut hens into serving sizes — ½ chicken per person.

3 Melt margarine and brush all over chicken halves.

4 Place flour, bread crumbs, salt, pepper, and paprika into a paper or plastic bag. Mix well. Put in one half of a chicken at a time, shaking bag so that all its parts are well covered.

5 Place into baking pan. Bake for 20 minutes. Turn chicken over and baste every 20 minutes to brown all over. Check chicken for taste and to see if ready. If not, bake for 15 minutes longer. Be careful not to overbake.

This recipe is good with matzah stuffing, asparagus, and carrots.

Chicken Cutlets

Here's an idea for a very fast meal.

1 Put cutlets on a wooden board and pound with a mallet to flatten to about ⅓" thickness.

Wash cutlets and leave them wet, so that flour will stick to them. (Use ice water, if you can; it keeps the breading from coming off.)

2 Preheat oven to 350°F.

3 Beat egg in a soup plate, adding a few Tbs. of water if needed to increase amount of liquid. Place flour on one flat plate and matzah meal or bread crumbs on another flat plate.

You can mix the seasoning with the bread crumbs; you can season the cutlets before you dip them into the flour; or you can season the beaten egg.

4 After dipping cutlets into the flour, dip them into the egg and then into the matzah meal or bread crumbs. For thicker breading, dip into the flour and egg and then again into the flour and egg, and finally into the matzah meal or bread crumbs.

5 In hot oil in a large skillet, brown cutlets for 2 minutes on each side over a medium-low flame. (Fry for twice as long if you're not going to bake them.) Remove the cutlets to a paper towel to absorb the oil.

6 Place the cutlets on a baking sheet or a shallow pan. Bake for a total of 10-12 minutes, turning the cutlets after 5 minutes.

2-3 chicken cutlets,
with fat removed

1-2 eggs
(or ¼ cup egg substitute)

5 Tbs. flour

**5 Tbs. matzah meal
or bread crumbs**

Salt and pepper to taste

Garlic powder to taste
(optional)

Paprika

2-3 Tbs. oil for sautéing

Chicken cutlets, fried or baked, are good with a fresh vegetable salad, a cooked vegetable such as cauliflower or Brussels sprouts, and potatoes or rice pilaf.

Baked Chicken Cutlets

2-3 chicken cutlets

Salt and pepper to taste

½ cup fine bread crumbs

Garlic powder to taste

A fast recipe that's healthier than frying.

Two to three cutlets will give you two portions.

1 Preheat oven to 350°F.

2 Wash and dry cutlets on a paper towel. Rub them lightly with margarine. Season both sides with salt, pepper, and garlic powder, and dip in bread crumbs.

3 Place in a shallow baking dish in oven for 25-40 minutes (depending on thickness). Turn after 15 minutes.

Check to see if more margarine is needed. Serve hot.

If cutlets get dried out, make a White Sauce to pour over them.

Chicken Cutlets
in Sweet and Sour Sauce

1 Place 3-4 Tbs. flour into a paper or plastic bag. Add salt, pepper, garlic powder, and paprika. Mix well.

2 Place a few bite-size pieces of chicken cutlets at a time into bag. Shake well to coat.

3 Heat oil in frying pan and sauté chicken on both sides. Place pieces on a paper towel to absorb oil. Set aside.

Sauce:

4 Pour 2 cups of boiling water into a medium-sized pot. Add sugar, salt, pepper, citric acid or lemon juice, and mix well. Check for taste.

5 Chop onion, and sauté with mushrooms.

6 Add sautéed onions, mushrooms, and the chicken cutlet pieces to sauce. Bring to a boil, reduce to simmer and let it all cook for 20 minutes or until the cutlet pieces are soft. Stir occasionally.

To thicken sauce, combine 1-2 tsp. cornstarch with about ¼ cup cold water and mix well. Add mixture to sauce and stir well until thickened.

Serve over white or brown rice. Good with broccoli, carrots, and a fresh vegetable salad.

Cutlets:

¾-1 lb. chicken cutlets, cut into 1¼" bite-size cubes

3-4 Tbs. flour

1 tsp. salt

⅛ tsp. pepper, to taste

½ tsp. garlic powder

½ tsp. paprika

2-3 Tbs. oil, or more

Sauce:

2 cups boiling water

¾-1 Tbs. sugar

½ tsp. salt

Dash of pepper, to taste

Pinch of citric acid (sour salt)
or 1-1½ Tbs. lemon juice, or to taste

1 onion

½ 4-oz. can sliced mushrooms

Best Chicken Patties

1 lb. chicken cutlets
or 1 lb. ground chicken

1-2 cloves garlic

1 egg

½-1 tsp. salt and dash of
pepper, or to taste

⅓ cup matzah meal

A few Tbs. water, to make
meat moist, if needed

Oil for frying

This recipe is tastiest made from fresh — not frozen — chicken. It makes 8-9 patties.

1 Chop cutlets by hand until of fine consistency, or use ground chicken from the butcher.

2 Beat the egg slightly. Mince the garlic. Then mix all ingredients together very well.

3 Wet hands. Form patties by making balls about 2" round, then flattening them to ½" thickness.

4 Fry in oil about 3-4 minutes on each side, until brown. Place on paper towel to absorb oil.

This dish can be eaten plain, like hamburgers, with mashed potatoes and whatever side dishes you choose, or with a sauce (optional).

Sauce:

Sauce:

2-3 Tbs. margarine

1½-2 cups boiling water

1 small onion

Oil for sautéing

½ tsp. salt

Dash of pepper

1-1½ tsp. flour

¼ cup cold water

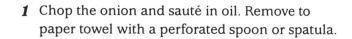

1 Chop the onion and sauté in oil. Remove to paper towel with a perforated spoon or spatula.

2 In a 3-quart pot, melt the margarine. Add the boiling water, sautéed onion, salt, and pepper.

3 Combine flour with ¼ cup cold water and mix well. Add to the pot and stir constantly while simmering over a low flame for 1-2 minutes. (If sauce is too thin, stir in ½-1½ tsp. cornstarch to thicken. If you want a darker color, stir in ¼-½ tsp. soy sauce or Kitchen Bouquet™.)

4 Carefully place patties into sauce and simmer 10-15 minutes. Stir a few times during cooking to keep onions from sticking to pot. Add 1-2 Tbs. water if sauce is too thick.

For a Sweet and Sour Sauce: Before putting patties into sauce, add 1 Tbs. sugar and 2 Tbs. lemon juice to the water. Adjust to your taste. Put in patties and simmer 10-15 minutes, as above.

Broiled Chicken or Turkey Patties

1 Preheat broiler to 400°F.

1 lb. chopped chicken
or turkey

2 Beat the egg and mix all ingredients except margarine together, chopping them in a wooden bowl.

1 egg

1 small onion

1-2 cloves garlic

3 Form round patties: Start by wetting hands or rubber gloves, if you wear them. Spoon out enough chopped meat to form a round ball about 1½", then flatten to make a patty about 2½" wide by ½" thick.

⅓ cup matzah meal

1 Tbs. onion soup mix
or ⅓ medium onion,
chopped plus 1 tsp. salt

Pepper and garlic powder,
to taste

4 Rub about 1 Tbs. of parve margarine into a broiling pan. Place meat patties onto the pan, and dot each patty with a small pat of margarine.

Margarine

5 Broil for 4 minutes, checking after 2 minutes for medium-rare, 5 minutes for well-done. Turn patties, baste with melted fat, and broil 1-2 minutes more. Do not overcook. Place on a paper towel to absorb oil.

For fried chicken or turkey patties:

Make meat patties as above. In a large skillet, fry each side in oil until brown. Place on paper towel to absorb oil before serving.

TURKEY
DISHES

You can buy any part of a turkey you like best,
or you can buy the whole bird, either frozen or fresh.
For one or two people it pays to buy just what you like,
such as the drumsticks, the thigh, or the breast.
Turkey is comparatively inexpensive, healthy,
and a good change from chicken.

♦   ♦   ♦   ♦   ♦   ♦   ♦   ♦   ♦

After many experiments, I have found the best way to roast a turkey. Season the turkey according to whatever recipe you are following. Put the turkey into the oven for three minutes at 450°F.

Reduce the oven temperature to 325°F and wrap the turkey in heavy aluminum foil. Roast breast-side down for 2-2½ hours, depending on the size of the turkey. Assuming it is 10 pounds, you can figure 20 minutes of roasting per pound, which would make this 200 minutes, or about 3½ hours. After 2 hours you still have 1½ hours to brown the turkey. Open the foil. Turn the bird over every 30 minutes and baste it every 20 minutes.

To test if the turkey is ready, you can use the same method as for chickens: Prick the thigh with a fork. If the juices that come out are red or pink, it is not done yet. If the juices are colorless, the turkey is done. You can also pry off a piece of the meat and taste it.

Another method is to buy a meat thermometer and insert it into the thigh at the beginning of roasting, being careful that it doesn't hit the bone. Leave it in until the temperature hits 180-185°F. Then your turkey is ready!

Stuffing

A lot of cooks make stuffing and fill the turkey cavity with it. It tastes good this way, because you get all the juices from the turkey saturating the stuffing, giving it that extra taste *(no denying that!)* but...

When stuffing a fowl, it is advisable to stuff it right before cooking it — that is, don't leave the stuffed bird in the refrigerator overnight. Moreover, after the meal, when you are putting away the leftovers, you should store the stuffing separately and not leave it in the cavity. Apparently, bacteria can breed rapidly under these circumstances and cause food poisoning.

Slicing the Turkey

Put the turkey on a carving board or large plate. It is best to allow it to cool for 15-20 minutes before slicing it. Cut off the wings and drumsticks and put them aside. Start to carve the breast in ⅛" thicknesses from the top of the breast near the neck and then down to the bottom. Cut as much as you want to eat or serve. Remove all the stuffing, if any. To store, cool the turkey, pack it in a plastic bag, and put it into the refrigerator.

Of all the different ways to cook turkey, I found the following two recipes to work best for me:

Delicious Roast Turkey

For a special holiday meal.

1 10-12 lb. turkey, fresh or frozen

1 lemon or orange

½ cup dry wine

½ cup orange juice

¼-½ cup margarine

2½-3 tsp. salt, or to taste

¼-½ tsp. pepper, or to taste

3-3½ tsp. garlic powder, or to taste

Paprika

1 Start to defrost the turkey, if frozen, the afternoon before you plan to roast it.

2 Clean the turkey and remove as much of the fat as you can, even under the skin, at the neck and the bottom, if you can reach it without tearing the skin. Cut off the tail (it is all fat). Remove the pin feathers. Wash the turkey and then dry it with paper towels.

3 Heat the oven to 450°F while you season the turkey.

4 Cut the lemon or orange in half, and rub each half all over the turkey, inside and outside, using up both halves. Mix wine and orange juice together, and pour over turkey.

Rub margarine all over the outside only. Sprinkle with salt, pepper, and garlic powder, inside and outside. Dust with paprika on the outside only.

5 Place the turkey on a piece of heavy-duty aluminum foil, large enough to cover it later. If you do not have heavy foil, double the regular foil.

6 Place turkey, breast down, on the heavy foil, in a large disposable foil pan or roasting pan. Leave uncovered for the first 3 minutes in the hot oven. This will sear in the juices.

7 Reduce temperature immediately to 325°F and wrap the foil all around turkey. Place breast down and seam up in the baking pan. Bake at 325°F for two hours.

8 Open foil and baste, baking uncovered until the turkey is done. Baste every 20 minutes and turn the turkey every 30 minutes until it is brown all over. (If the turkey begins to get too dark, cover it with foil again until it's fully cooked.)

9 Check to see if turkey is ready. When it is, remove from oven and cool for about 20 minutes before slicing.

This recipe is good with stuffing (see recipes), baked sweet potatoes, a cooked vegetable such as asparagus, string beans, or Brussels sprouts, and a potato kugel. Cranberry sauce is very tasty with the turkey.

Another Delicious Roast Turkey (with Stuffing)

**1 10-12 lb. fresh
or frozen turkey**

**½ cup vegetable oil,
or ¼ cup French dressing
mixed with ¼ cup oil**

2½-3 tsp. salt

¼-½ tsp. pepper

**4 tsp. garlic powder,
or enough to cover
outside and inside**

5-6 cups of stuffing
(see recipes pages 224-226)

1 Start to defrost the turkey, if frozen, the afternoon before you intend to cook it.

2 Heat oven to 325°F. Clean and prepare turkey, removing as much of the fat as you can.

3 Rub a lot of oil or French dressing mixed with oil, all over turkey, inside and outside. Sprinkle turkey with salt, pepper, and garlic powder.

4 Fill the cavity with the stuffing. Sew up skin on each end with a doubled strand of white thread. If you choose not to stuff turkey, place the stuffing in a greased casserole dish and bake separately.

5 Bake turkey uncovered, about 3½-4 hours, depending on the size (20 minutes per pound). Baste turkey every 25 minutes and turn every 50 minutes to 1 hour. If turkey starts to get too dark, cover with foil.

When storing the turkey after the meal, remove all the stuffing from the cavity and store it separately.

This recipe is good with cranberry sauce, sweet potatoes, and carrots.

Turkey Legs, Wings, Breasts, etc.

This recipe is good if you are roasting a part of a turkey.

Season the turkey parts with ⅓ of the amount of seasonings that you would use for a whole turkey, or to taste. If the part is only 2½ pounds, it should take 1½-2 hours to cook. Test to see if the turkey is done by pulling off a small piece of meat with a fork and tasting it.

The breast of the turkey tends to be very dry and many people prefer to drench it with a sauce after it has been cooked.

Turkey Cutlets

Some butchers now have something new: They make cutlets from a very large turkey drumstick, with the bone in the center, or from the breast. If your butcher has these, try them.

Turkey cutlets

Salt and pepper, to taste

Garlic powder, to taste

Margarine

1 Rub cutlet with very little margarine, then season with salt, pepper, and garlic powder.

2 Put into broiler, 4-6 minutes each side, or until soft.

These cutlets are tasty and very quick to prepare. Good with mashed potatoes, canned or frozen sweet peas, and fresh vegetable salad.

Turkey Leg Pot Roast

1-3 turkey legs
(or other parts)

1-2 cloves garlic
or 1-1½ tsp. garlic powder

1-1½ tsp. salt, or to taste

1-2 dashes pepper

½ tsp. paprika

1 medium onion

1-2 Tbs. oil

1½ cups water

2-3 potatoes

3-4 carrots

1 Preheat oven to 400°F.

2 Wash turkey legs, remove as much fat as you can, and dry on a paper towel.

3 Season: First rub turkey legs with minced garlic, if using. Otherwise, just season with salt, pepper, and garlic powder. Dust with paprika. Set aside.

4 Chop onion and sauté in oil. Remove and drain. Place in a heavy pot or Dutch oven.

5 Boil 1½ cups of water, add to pot, and then place turkey parts into water. Bake for 1-1¼ hours, covered. Reduce heat to 350°F, and bake another 15 minutes.

6 Peel potatoes and carrots. Cut potatoes into quarters; cut carrots through the middle into 2¼" lengths. Add potatoes and carrots to pot. Baste vegetables and turkey every 15 minutes, adding a little water if necessary. Bake another 30-45 minutes. Total baking time: 2-2½ hours.

Optional: Before serving, place turkey legs in a shallow baking dish and put under broiler at 500°F for 2 minutes on each side. If you are using breast, and not legs, do not broil it — it will get too dry.

Leftover Turkey in White Sauce

If you are tired of eating the same turkey again and again — try this recipe for a pleasant change!

White Sauce
(see pg. 230)

Leftover cooked turkey

1 medium onion

1-2 Tbs. oil

½-1 cup Minute Rice™

1 Make a *White Sauce* (see recipe) in a 3-4 quart pot and set aside.

2 Chop the onion, and sauté it in oil. Add half to the white sauce, and mix. Reserve the other half.

3 Cut up cooked turkey into bite-size pieces 1-1¼" long, put them into white sauce, and let simmer about 10 minutes, until turkey is hot, stirring often. Adjust taste.

4 In another pot, cook ½-1 cup of Minute Rice™ according to the directions on the package. Mix other half of sautéed onion into the cooked rice.

Serve rice covered with the turkey/white sauce mixture. If serving company, place rice in a serving dish and turkey-white sauce mixture in another dish. Serve hot.

Hints & Tips

Instead of rice, you can use Barley Shapes with Mushrooms and Onion (see recipe). This recipe is good with broccoli and sweet peas.

Leftover Turkey
in Sweet and Sour Sauce

1 Make the same *White Sauce* as in *Leftover Turkey* recipe above, adding a pinch of citric acid and a little sugar while cooking the white sauce. All other ingredients are the same as the above recipe.

2 Adjust to your taste and add the bite-size turkey pieces. Let it all simmer for 10-20 minutes, stirring often. Serve with side dishes as above.

Turkey Salad

See recipe for Chicken or Turkey Salad Sandwich, pg. 284.

Serve with boiled or mashed potatoes, green peas, and fresh vegetable salad.

For lunch, make turkey salad sandwiches. They're always a big hit, with vegetable salad, half-sour pickles, and hot tea.

DUCK
DISHES

Duck is one of my favorite dishes.
It has a very sweet taste and makes a delicious meal
to serve your guests on a special occasion.

♦　♦　♦　♦　♦　♦　♦　♦　♦

Roast Duck

Since duck contains a lot of fat, it is not healthy.
However, this recipe reduces some of the fat.

1 Preheat oven to 350°F.

2 Remove as much fat as you can while cleaning
the duck. Wash, then dry with paper towels.

3 Put duck into a roasting pan in the oven,
covered. After 20 minutes, prick skin all over
with a fork to let fat escape. Spill out melted fat,
then put the duck back into oven for another 25
minutes. Spill out all fat again. *Let cool for about*
10 minutes so that you can season it without
burning your hands.

4 Cut the orange in half and rub the inside and
outside of the duck with it. Then sprinkle the
garlic powder.

5 Dice the onion. Boil the water and add it, with
the diced onion, to the pan.

6 Bake, covered, for another 30 minutes. Remove
cover and add a little more water, if needed.
Bake for another 35-45 minutes.

1 duck, 4-5 lbs.

1 orange

1½ tsp. garlic powder

1 small onion

1 cup water

Use no salt:
Duck is quite salty

Total cooking time should be about 1¾-2 hours. Check often during the last ½ hour to see if done. Turn duck to brown evenly during the last hour. Do *not* overbake, as it will dry out the duck meat.

To make sauce, see recipe in *Sauces and Gravies*.

This recipe is delicious with potato kugel or sweet potatoes, broccoli soufflé, and a fresh vegetable salad.

Sweet Orange Glazed Duck

1 duck, 4-5 lbs.

½ **cup apricot, peach, or orange preserves**

¼ **cup honey**

1-2 Tbs. kosher brandy
peach or orange-flavored, to match the preserve

1 Roast duck for 1½ hours according to instructions of previous recipe.

2 Mix preserves, honey, and brandy together. Mix glaze well until smooth and to your taste. Coat duck all over outside, lightly, and return to oven for 10-15 minutes, uncovered.

Alternative:

Into commercial duck sauce, mix brandy and a little honey (optional), to your taste. Coat duck lightly, and return to oven for 10-15 minutes more, uncovered.

BEEF DISHES

♦ ♦ ♦ ♦ ♦ ♦ ♦ ♦ ♦

Square-Cut Roast

1 Preheat oven to 350°F. Wash meat and dry with paper towel. Rub meat with vegetable oil, then with fresh garlic, minced.

2 Put meat into roasting pan. Sprinkle with onion soup mix or sautéed onions. Season with pepper and dust lightly with garlic powder and paprika.

3 Boil the water and pour into pan. Cover roasting pan with foil. Bake meat for 1 hour, and then remove from the oven and slice. Return meat to oven and continue baking another 1-1½ hours. Check occasionally. Add more water, if needed. Adjust seasoning to taste.

Good with potato pancakes or mashed potatoes mixed with fried onions, asparagus and carrots, and fresh vegetable salad.

2-2½ lb. lean, square-cut beef

Vegetable oil

2 cloves garlic

⅓-½ envelope onion soup mix or 1 medium onion, chopped and sautéed

Pepper, to taste

Garlic powder, to taste

1 tsp. paprika to dust meat

1 cup water

Meat can be sliced easily after the first hour of cooking and then returned to the oven, or after it's completely done and has cooled off for about 20-30 minutes. Use a very sharp knife, to avoid tearing meat.

Hints & Tips

Lean Brisket

2½ lbs. brisket
*For larger pieces of meat,
increase all ingredients
proportionately*

1-2 tsp. margarine

**⅓ envelope onion
soup mix
or 1 medium onion**

½ cup ketchup

3-4 Tbs. apricot jelly

¼-½ cup warm water

½ onion

Brisket is a very lean cut of beef and is quite tasty, but it is often packaged and sold in large cuts of five pounds and up! Therefore, you may have a hard time finding a small piece for two meals.

You may have to buy a larger piece, cut off about half of it to cook two or three good portions, and freeze the rest to cook another time. Alternatively, you can cook the large piece, use part of it and freeze the rest. If buying from a butcher, he can cut it for you and sell just a piece, or at least save you the trouble of cutting it yourself.

1 Preheat oven to 350°F.

2 Wash brisket. Dry with paper towel. Lightly grease a medium size roasting pan with margarine.

3 Chop and sauté onion, or use onion soup powder, and mix with ketchup and apricot jelly. Add a little warm water to thin mixture somewhat. (If onion soup mix is not used, add 1-1½ tsp. salt and a dash of pepper to chopped onion.)

4 Spread half of mixture on bottom of roasting pan, the rest on top of brisket.

5 Cover and bake for 1 hour. Remove from oven and cut into slices. Return to pan, cover and bake another 1½ hours, or until soft. Check occasionally to see if more water is needed. Sauce should be slightly thick, but flowing.

Good with potato kugel, string beans, and glazed carrots.

Oven Pot Roast

1 Preheat oven to 400°F.

2 Wash meat and remove as much of the fat as you can.

3 Brown meat by putting in roasting pan in hot oven for 15 minutes on each side. Take out of oven, and season meat with salt, pepper, and garlic powder. Dust with paprika.

4 Chop onion and sauté until golden. Spread on meat. Boil water and add enough to come just below top of meat.

5 Reduce heat to 350°F and bake 1 hour.

6 Remove meat from oven. Cut into slices and return to oven, adding more hot water if needed.

7 Peel 2-3 potatoes, quarter them, and add to roasting pan. Bake 1 more hour.

Total roasting time: About 3 hours.

2½ lb. piece of beef
Shoulder roast, end of beef, or shell roast

1-1½ tsp. salt

Dash of pepper

2 tsp. garlic powder

Paprika

1 large onion

1½-2 cups water

2-3 potatoes
(optional)

Pot Roast on Top of Stove

2½-3 lb. meat
*Brisket, deckel, shell roast,
or any other red meat*

3 Tbs. vegetable oil

1 tsp. salt, or to taste

**A few dashes of pepper,
or to taste**

1½-2 tsp. garlic powder

1 tsp. paprika

1 large onion

1½-2 cups water

2 cloves garlic

A few potatoes
(optional)

1 Wash meat after removing the fat.

2 Put 2-3 Tbs. oil in a frying pan or a heavy pot, and brown meat in hot oil on both sides. Remove and season with salt, pepper, and garlic powder. Sprinkle with paprika.

3 Chop onion and sauté. Place into meat pot. Boil 1½-2 cups of water and pour into pot. Make cuts in the garlic cloves and place them into the pot.

4 Bring to a boil, reduce heat and simmer the pot roast for 1 hour. Keep pot covered during cooking with the lid slightly askew.

5 Remove meat from pot, slice, and return to pot. Add more water if needed. Let simmer for another 1-2 hours until meat is soft.

6 Peel and quarter the potatoes, if using, and add to pot 35 minutes before roast is finished. Check for taste. Discard whole garlic.

Good with a cooked vegetable such as asparagus, Brussels sprouts, green beans or carrots, and potatoes cooked in any way.

Another Good Pot Roast

1 Preheat oven to 350°F.

2 Wash meat and dry in paper towel. Remove any excess fat.

3 Brown meat in pot on top of stove for about 15 minutes on each side. Take meat out, season with salt, pepper, garlic powder, and paprika, to your taste. Place in roasting pan and set aside.

4 Chop onion and sauté until golden. Boil 1 cup of water and add to meat with chopped onion.

5 Put in the oven and bake, covered, for 2-2½ hours. Check every 30-45 minutes, adding water if needed.

6 If you like, peel and quarter 2-3 potatoes and add them for the last 25-35 minutes of cooking. Some cuts of meat require 3 hours of cooking.

2½ lb. beef
Shoulder roast, shoulder steak, end of beef, or square cut

1½ tsp. salt, or to taste

3-4 dashes of pepper, or to taste

1-½ tsp. garlic powder, or to taste

1 tsp. paprika, or to taste

1 onion

1 cup water

2-3 potatoes
(optional)

Plain and Delicious Roast Beef

2½-3 lb. beef
Shell roast, strip roast, or silver tip roast

Vegetable oil

½ envelope onion soup mix, or to taste

1-1½ tsp. garlic powder

1-1½ tsp. paprika

½-1 cup water
or ⅓ cup dry white wine plus ½ cup water

1 Preheat oven to 350°F.

2 Rub vegetable oil all over meat, then season with onion soup mix, garlic powder, and paprika.

3 Put meat onto heavy foil in roasting pan. Carefully add ½ cup or more boiling water (or wine/water combination) before closing foil tightly around the roast and the liquid. Bake 1½ hours.

4 Remove from oven, slice meat, and rewrap. Bake 1½ hours more or until soft. Check every 45 minutes, adding more water if needed. Test by cutting a piece of meat off and tasting it. Check seasoning.

Good with rice pilaf, broccoli, and carrots.

Stew with Tomato Sauce

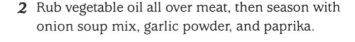

1½-2 lb. chuck, cut into 1" pieces

1 tsp. salt, to taste

⅛ tsp. pepper, to taste

Vegetable oil or other fat

1 onion

½-¾ cup water

1 8-oz. can tomato sauce

3 carrots

2 potatoes

1 Wash meat and season with salt and pepper.

2 Brown meat in vegetable oil or any other parve fat. Remove from pan and set aside.

3 In same oil, sauté onion, chopped or sliced thin. When done, add water and tomato sauce. Stir in meat and simmer for 1½ hours.

4 Peel and cut up carrots and potatoes. Add to meat.

5 Continue to simmer until vegetables are done. The meat should be ready, but if not, take out carrots and potatoes and let meat simmer until tender. Put back carrots and potatoes. Add water as necessary. *Serve hot with vegetables.*

STEAKS
AND CHOPS

The important thing to remember
when buying steak is that the quality of the meat
has a lot to do with the taste.
Choose the First Cut, if possible.
It may be a little more expensive,
but you will get the taste you want.
I've found, though, that the first cut of beef chuck
is quite good and less expensive than other steaks.
Also, be sure to choose the leaner steaks with less fat.

◆　　◆　　◆　　◆　　◆　　◆　　◆　　◆　　◆

All steaks taste good broiled in a broiler. The thinner steaks, ½" or less, can also be pan-fried on top of the stove. Thin steaks can be breaded as well. (To thin a steak, place it onto a wooden slicing board and pound it all over with a mallet until you have the thickness you want.)

The broiler or frying pan should be heated before the meat is placed into it for cooking. Steaks require only a small amount of greasing of the pan, since the fat from the meat melts, too. After the steaks are done, pour out the fat that has run off.

Most steaks require only a few minutes of broiling or frying on each side. They can be seasoned before cooking, but hold back on the salt until after the steak is cooked. For medium rare, the thinner cuts (½"-¾" thick), broiled four to five inches from the flame, take only about three minutes on each side. Medium-well takes about five minutes on each side, and well-done about eight minutes on each side. Since only you know how you like your steak, you will have to check it often during cooking and turn it frequently.

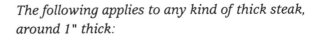

Thick Broiled Steaks

Thick steaks

1 Tbs. vegetable oil

1 Tbs. soy sauce

1 tsp. garlic powder

The following applies to any kind of thick steak, around 1" thick:

1 Rub each steak with oil and soy sauce, and sprinkle with garlic powder. Place each steak into a plastic bag and close well. Put them on a plate to marinate in the refrigerator for 2½-3 hours, turning the bagged steaks every ½-¾ hour.

2 Preheat oven or broiler to highest setting. Remove steaks from plastic bags and place on a broiler pan. Broil 4 minutes on each side for rare, 7 minutes for medium, and 10 minutes on each side for well-done. Check often.

You probably won't need salt, since soy sauce is quite salty already.

Other condiments:

Barbeque sauce can also be used to season the steaks. Simply spread the barbeque sauce on top of the steak and broil it according to the time that you like (rare, medium, or well-done). Then turn the steak, spread the barbeque sauce onto that side, and broil until done.

Some people spread tomato ketchup on the steak when they eat it; others like mustard or steak sauce. I eat it plain — the marinade and seasoning applied to the meat satisfy my taste.

Minute Steaks

1 Preheat broiler. Wash steak, and dry on a paper towel.

2 Rub each side of the steak with a little oil, 1 tsp. of soy sauce, and garlic cloves squeezed through your garlic press or garlic powder.

3 Broil 2-3 minutes each side or until steak is done to your liking.

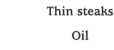

Thin steaks

Oil

Soy sauce

Fresh or powdered garlic

 ## Lamb Chops

Lamb chops are usually broiled, but since they are quite fatty, do not use any oil to rub into them.

1 Season with soy sauce and garlic powder.

2 Broil about 5-6 minutes on each side for medium-well and approximately 7-8 minutes on each side for well-done, checking every 2 minutes.

Lamb chops

Soy sauce

Garlic powder

 ## Fried Veal Chops

1 Use one or two first-cut veal chops. Put the oil into a heavy frying pan and preheat.

2 Season steaks with pepper and garlic powder or a minced or pressed fresh clove of garlic, mix it with 1 tsp. of soy sauce, and rub it into the meat.

3 Brown on both sides in frying pan, turning chops every few minutes. Fry for 2 minutes on each side for medium-rare, 5 minutes on each

Veal chops

2-3 tsp. oil

Pepper

Fresh or powdered garlic

Soy sauce

side for well-done. Turn meat often, so it doesn't burn. Discard melted fat.

Good served with sautéed onions, potatoes of any kind, and broccoli.

Breaded Veal Chops

Veal chops

Pepper

Garlic powder

Paprika

Oil for frying

Breading:

4-5 Tbs. flour

4-5 Tbs. matzah meal

Salt

Pepper

Garlic powder

Paprika

1 egg

1 Wash meat and dry on a paper towel.

2 Season veal chops with a few dashes of pepper or to taste, ½ tsp. garlic powder, and sprinkle with paprika.

Breading:

3 Put flour on a flat plate. On a second plate put matzah meal mixed well with salt, pepper, garlic powder, and paprika. In a soup bowl, beat the egg slightly.

4 Heat frying pan with 2 Tbs. vegetable oil.

5 Dip seasoned veal chops into the flour, then into the egg, and finally into the matzah meal.

6 Place breaded chops into hot frying pan, reduce heat and fry until done on one side. Turn and fry on other side (about 3-4 minutes each side), adding more oil if needed.

The same method can be used to bread and fry any other type of meat as well.

Good with mashed potatoes, broccoli, and green peas or carrots.

VEAL DISHES

Veal Stew

1 Remove fat from veal pieces. Wash and dry in paper towel. Set aside.

2 Chop onion and sauté in oil until golden. Remove onions from oil and put aside on separate plate and, in the same pan, sauté meat over a low flame for about 10-15 minutes.

3 Season meat with salt, pepper, and paprika and mix well. Add sautéed onions.

4 Boil the water and add to the meat, along with the garlic. Simmer over very low flame for 30 minutes.

5 Julienne-cut red or green pepper into 1" slices and add to stew. Simmer another 30-40 minutes, checking every 15 minutes for taste and to see if more water is needed. If so, add ⅓ cup water at a time.

To thicken sauce, stir in a mixture of 1-2 Tbs. flour or cornstarch and some cold water 15 minutes before veal is done or after about 45 minutes of cooking, only if needed.

Good with string beans, cauliflower, and any kind of potatoes.

1½ lb. veal,
cut into 1½-2" chunks

1 large onion

Oil for sautéing

1 tsp. salt, or to taste

3-4 dashes of pepper

1 tsp. paprika

2 cups boiling water

1 clove garlic
(optional)

1 medium-size red
or green sweet pepper

1-1½ Tbs. flour
or cornstarch

Quick Fried Veal Cutlets (Wiener Schnitzel)

1-2 veal cutlets
(first cut)

Salt and pepper, to taste

4 Tbs. flour

1 egg

5-6 Tbs. matzah meal

Oil for frying

1 Pound cutlets with a mallet to ¼" thickness. Season to taste with salt and pepper.

2 Put flour and matzah meal onto separate plates. Beat egg in a soup plate. Dip both sides of cutlets into flour, then into egg, then into matzah meal.

For thicker breading, dip cutlets into flour, then egg, then flour and egg again, and finally into the matzah meal.

3 Fry in hot oil in frying pan, over medium to low heat, about 3-4 minutes each side.

Baked Veal Cutlets

1-2 veal cutlets with bone
(first cut)

Salt and pepper to taste

1 clove fresh garlic

Paprika to taste

1 The night before, mix salt and pepper to taste with minced garlic and paprika. Rub into cutlets on both sides. Cover and refrigerate overnight.

2 Next day, preheat oven to 350°F. Pour off any water that may have accumulated. Put cutlets onto a baking sheet and bake for 10 minutes. Turn, bake for another 5-10 minutes, or longer, if needed. Check often. *Do not overbake or meat becomes leathery!*

Good with barley shape mix (see Side Dishes) or french-fried potatoes, small sweet peas (frozen or canned), fresh or frozen corn on the cob, and a fresh vegetable salad.

More Baked Veal Cutlets

1 Heat oven to 350°F.

2 Pour cornflakes into a paper or plastic bag, and crush with hands or mallet to make small crumbs. Add salt, pepper, and paprika, and mix well. Pour onto a large plate.

3 Rub cutlets with minced garlic. Spread lightly with mayonnaise and dip into seasoned cornflakes.

4 Grease a baking pan lightly. Place cutlets on pan and bake 8-10 minutes on each side, until soft. Check every few minutes. *Do not overcook, or cutlets will dry out.*

Good with mashed potatoes and sweet peas (canned or frozen).

4-5 Tbs. cornflakes

½ tsp. salt

Pinch of pepper

½ tsp. paprika

2 veal cutlets

1 clove fresh garlic

1-2 Tbs. mayonnaise

Oil or margarine
for greasing pan

Veal and Peppers

1½ lbs. veal,
cut into bite-size cubes
(about 1¼"x1")

4-5 Tbs. flour

Salt and pepper, to taste

½-¾ tsp. paprika

Oil to sauté

1 medium onion,
chopped

1½-2 cups water

½-1 sweet red pepper

½-1 sweet green pepper

6 oz. fresh mushrooms,
sliced, or 1 4-oz. can
sliced mushrooms

1 Wash meat and dry on a paper towel. Remove any skin or fat.

2 Put flour into a paper or plastic bag. Add salt, pepper, and paprika and mix well. Put a few cubes of meat into bag at a time and shake to cover.

3 Chop onion. In large skillet, in hot oil, sauté meat, then onion.

4 Transfer both into a pot and add 1½ cups of boiling water. Season with salt and pepper to taste. Bring to a boil, reduce to a simmer. Cook for 1¼-1½ hours.

5 Julienne-cut peppers into 1½" lengths, and slice mushrooms, if using fresh. Add peppers and mushrooms to pot. Cook for another ½ hour or until meat is soft. Sauce should be slightly thick, not watery.

To thicken sauce, mix ½ Tbs. (or more) flour with a little cold water until smooth. Add to pot, simmer, and stir another few minutes until sauce is thicker.

Serve over hot noodles or barley shapes, with broccoli on the side. (See recipes, Side Dishes.)

GROUND MEAT DISHES

*All ground meat dishes taste best
when made from fresh meat, rather than frozen.
When the recipe calls for ground beef,
you can substitute ground chicken, turkey, or veal
for part or all of it.*

♦ ♦ ♦ ♦ ♦ ♦ ♦ ♦ ♦

 ## Hamburgers

1 Combine meat with egg, chopped onion, matzah meal, garlic, salt and pepper. Mix well. If dry, add a small amount of water to moisten.

1-1½ lbs. ground meat

1 egg
(optional)

2 Wet hands. Form meat into balls about 2½" in diameter. Flatten to about ½" thickness.

1 small onion, chopped

⅓-½ cup matzah meal

3 In a skillet, heat the oil and fry hamburgers over a medium-low flame until brown on both sides, about 3 minutes on the first side and 2 minutes on the second. Place on paper towel to absorb oil.

1-2 cloves garlic, minced or ½ tsp. garlic powder

1 tsp. salt, or to taste

Dash of pepper

Oil for frying

4 For baked hamburgers, do not fry. Just place them on a greased baking sheet, dot each one with a small pat of margarine, and bake at 350°F for 30-45 minutes.

Margarine
(for baked patties)

Good with mashed potatoes, green peas, and carrots. Leftovers can be reheated the next day or can be used to make very tasty sandwiches for lunch.

Broiled Veal or Beef Patties

1 lb. ground veal
or any other ground meat

1 small onion, chopped

Salt and pepper, to taste

1-2 cloves garlic

1 egg, beaten
(optional)

⅓-½ cup matzah meal

Margarine

1 Preheat broiler to 450°F.

2 Mix all ingredients together except the margarine, chopping them in a wooden bowl.

3 Form patties: Start by wetting hands or rubber gloves, if you wear them. Spoon out enough ground meat to form round balls about 2½" in diameter, then flatten to make patties about 2½" wide by ½"-¾" thick.

4 Rub about 1-2 Tbs. of parve margarine into a broiling pan, place meat patties onto the pan, and dot each patty with a small pat of margarine.

5 Broil 3 minutes for medium-rare, 4-5 minutes for well-done. Turn patties, baste with melted fat, and broil 1-2 minutes more. *Do not overcook.* Place on a paper towel to absorb oil.

Meat Loaf

1 lb. ground beef chuck

1 lb. ground turkey breast
or chicken breast

1 small onion

1 egg, beaten

Salt and pepper to taste

½ cup uncooked oats
or matzah meal

¾-1 cup tomato juice

1-2 cloves garlic

Margarine

1 Preheat oven to 350°F.

2 Chop onion and finely mince garlic. Mix all ingredients thoroughly. Grease a 8"x4"x2" loaf pan and pat meat mixture in.

3 Bake for 45 minutes to 1 hour. Let cool 5-6 minutes before slicing. Makes 6 servings.

Meatballs in Tomato Sauce

1 Chop onion and combine with meat, egg, seasonings, and matzah meal. Form into round balls the size of large walnuts.

2 Heat the oil in a frying pan. Brown meatballs on all sides in hot oil, and place on paper towel, to drain excess oil.

3 Put tomato sauce and water into a medium-size pot. Make a cut in the garlic clove to let juices come out and put garlic into pot. Add meat balls and bring to boil. Reduce to simmer and cover the pot with the lid slightly askew to allow steam to escape. Cook 30-45 minutes, adding more water if necessary. Discard garlic.

Good with spaghetti, rice pilaf, or barley shapes and mushroom mix.

1-1½ lbs. ground meat

1 small onion

1 egg, beaten

1-1½ tsp. salt, or to taste

⅛ tsp. pepper, or to taste

½-¾ tsp. garlic powder

⅓-½ cup matzah meal

Oil

1 8-oz. can tomato sauce plus ½ can water

1-2 cloves garlic, whole

FISH DISHES

Gefilte Fish (from scratch)

½ lb. yellow pike

½ lb. carp

½ lb. whitefish

1 medium onion

1-2 eggs

½ cup matzah meal

1-2 tsp. salt, or to taste

⅛ tsp. pepper

1½-2 Tbs. sugar

Stock:

1 large onion, cut up

1-2 carrots, sliced

1 stalk celery, sliced

1½-2 tsp. salt, or to taste

2 dashes of pepper,
or to taste

1-2 Tbs. sugar

6 cups water

This recipe is for Polish gefilte fish. Those who like Russian gefilte fish won't touch it. For them, take the sugar out of the recipe and put in more black pepper!

1 Grind fish and onion, or have it done in the fish store. (If you chop it yourself, first remove all the bones and skin.) Mix in remaining ingredients.

2 Wet hands and form large oval balls, 2½" long and 1½" thick. Put them aside while you prepare the stock.

Stock:

3 Pour the water into a large pot and bring to a boil. Place onions, carrots, and celery into pot. Add salt, pepper, and sugar, and bring to a boil again. Add the fish balls gently, one by one, and return to simmer (very low flame).

4 Cook for 1½ hours in covered pot with the lid slightly askew. After ¾ hour, check taste and adjust seasonings, if needed.

5 Remove fish balls to a plate, let cool, cover, and refrigerate. You will have about 15 pieces.

If stock is too watery, let it boil down for about another 10 minutes after you remove the fish, until you have about 2½-3 cups of fish sauce.

6 Discard celery and onion pieces; save carrots to decorate fish balls. Let stock cool, pour into a glass jar with a screw top, and refrigerate. This sauce will jell, if it's not too watery.

Serve fish cold, on a bed of lettuce, garnishing with carrot slices, if desired.

Gefilte Fish Balls from Frozen Loaf

This is faster than making them from scratch.

1 Defrost frozen gefilte fish loaf (it takes about 3-4 hours) and remove completely from its packaging. Place in a wooden chopping bowl.

2 If you wish to change the taste, you can do so by adding more sugar, salt, or pepper, according to your taste. Since it already has all the other ingredients, you don't need to add anything else. However, if the mixture is too watery, you must add more matzah meal, to make the consistency good for forming fish balls. Form fish balls as in the preceding recipe.

3 Place vegetables and a little salt into a pot filled with enough cold water to just cover fish balls. Bring to a boil.

4 Carefully add the fish balls to the boiling stock, reduce to simmer, and cook for 1½ hours, in a covered pot with the lid slightly askew.

5 Remove fish balls and carrot slices to a dry plate, let cool, cover, and refrigerate. If stock is too watery, let it boil down another ½ hour or until it's reduced to 2-3 cups. Remove remaining vegetables by pouring stock through a

1 frozen gefilte fish loaf

Matzah meal, as needed

1 carrot, sliced

1 medium onion, cut up

1½ tsp. salt, or to taste

⅛ tsp. pepper

1½-2 Tbs. sugar

1 stalk celery, sliced

strainer into a glass jar. If you like onions, you can put back some of the cooked onions into the strained stock. Refrigerate. Use the carrot slices to garnish the fish balls.

Gefilte Fish Loaf

1 frozen gefilte fish loaf

1 large onion

2 carrots

1 stalk of celery

1 tsp. salt, or to taste

1-2 dashes of pepper, or to taste

2 Tbs. sugar, or to taste

This takes even less time to prepare.

1 In a large pot, bring to a boil 5-6 cups of water, or enough to barely cover fish loaf (but don't put it in yet). Chop onion, slice carrots and celery, and add to pot with seasonings.

2 Reduce to simmer, and add fish loaf, *wrapped in its wax paper, seam of paper down.* Bring again to boil, reduce to lowest flame, and let simmer 1½-1¾ hours in a covered pot.

3 Remove fish loaf and place on a plate for 10 minutes to cool. Then open wax paper and let loaf cool to room temperature. Sprinkle with salt and pepper, if desired. Store in refrigerator in aluminum foil or in a flat plastic container with a cover. Keep the loaf in one piece, cutting slices as needed. Save carrots to garnish fish slices. This stock will be watery and will not jell.

4 If there is too much liquid after removing the fish, let stock boil down on a medium flame for 15-20 minutes. Cool to room temperature. Strain stock, discarding those vegetables that you don't want. Pour into a glass jar, cover, and refrigerate. *Serve fish cold.*

◆ ◆ ◆ ◆ ◆ ◆ ◆ ◆ ◆

Boiled and Poached Fish

*Boiling and poaching (simmering gently)
are the traditional methods of cooking fish
like carp, pike, whitefish, and whiting
for Shabbos and holidays.*

◆ ◆ ◆ ◆ ◆ ◆ ◆ ◆ ◆

Carp

This makes 2-3 portions.

1 Place the sliced or cut up vegetables on the bottom of a large pot. Place regular or winter carp on top of vegetables, and pour in enough cold water to just cover the fish (about 3 cups). Add salt, pepper, sugar, if using, and bay leaf.

4-6 pieces of carp
*have store cut them into
1" slices across*

1½-2 carrots

1 onion

2 stalks celery

1½ tsp. salt, or to taste

Dash or two of pepper

1½ Tbs. sugar
(optional)

1 bay leaf

2 Bring to a boil, reduce to simmer, and cook partially covered. Cook regular carp for 30-45 minutes. Winter carp needs only 12-20 minutes. Add more water, if needed (very little), and adjust taste. Fish is done if it flakes when touched with a fork.

3 Carefully remove fish with a wide spatula, so that it doesn't fall apart. Put it on a plate to cool, then cover and refrigerate.

4 Cool sauce, strain, and discard vegetables and bay leaf. Save carrots to garnish slices of fish. Sauce will not jell if there's too much water. To reduce amount of liquid, boil sauce down for 10-15 minutes more after removing fish and vegetables.

Whitefish and Pike

4 1½" slices of fish

1½-2 carrots

1 onion

1½ tsp. salt, or to taste

Dash or two of pepper

1½ Tbs. sugar
(optional)

1 bay leaf

2½ cups water

1 First boil all ingredients *except* fish for 10-14 minutes. Place fish into the boiling stock. Reduce to a simmer and cook 10-15 minutes in a partially covered pot.

2 Check fish; if it flakes, it's ready. With a wide spatula, remove fish to a plate. Let cool and refrigerate.

3 Cool stock, strain, pour into a glass jar, cover and refrigerate. Whitefish stock will jell only if you use no more than 2-2½ cups of water for 4 slices of fish.

 # Whiting

This is a soft fish that takes very little time to cook.

1 Use several fish steaks, depending on size. Wash fish and save the heads to cook along with fish.

2 Cook the same way as *Whitefish* (above), but after boiling all other ingredients, vegetables and seasoning, simmer fish for only about 5 minutes. Check to see if fish flakes easily, then remove. Adjust seasoning, if needed.

3 Transfer fish to a separate plate and remove the inside membrane while fish is still fairly hot. (This can also be done before cooking fish; it comes off easily then, too. It will not come off after fish is cold.) Boiling the sauce with the heads alone for 5-10 minutes more helps to make it jell.

4 Let stock cool and pour it into a glass jar and cover. This stock will jell.

Salmon with Vegetables

This recipe can also be made with halibut, tile-fish, or cod.

2-3 slices of salmon fillet

¼-⅓ head of broccoli, florets only

¼ head of cauliflower

1 carrot

1 stalk celery

1 small onion

1 potato

1 bay leaf

1 tsp. salt, or to taste

Dash of pepper

1 Fill half a 4-quart pot with cold water. Slice carrots and celery, cut up onion, and cut potato into cubes. Add to water with seasonings. Bring to a boil, lower the flame, and cook 15 minutes or until vegetables are soft enough to eat.

2 Turn off flame, place salmon into water immediately, cover pot and set aside for 6-10 minutes, until fish flakes when tested with a fork. Discard bay leaf and remove fish from water. Good hot or cold.

Serve sauce and vegetables separately or together with fish. Fish may also be served with mashed potatoes and small sweet green peas.

Baked and Broiled Fish

Any fish can be baked or broiled.
Both methods are much healthier than frying.

General Instructions for Baking and Broiling Fish

All types of fish should be seasoned before you cook them, unless the recipe specifies differently.

The important thing about both baking and broiling is not to overcook the fish, since overbaking or overbroiling will dry out the fish meat and may spoil the meal. Therefore, checking often during cooking will help. To see if the fish is ready, pry with a fork; if the fish flakes, it's ready.

Broiling

Rub pan with about ½-1½ tsp. softened butter or margarine, depending on size of pan and fish. Dot the top of the fish with a few small pieces of margarine or butter.

Broiling fish takes much less time than baking. Fillets take only 4-5 minutes. Place rack about 3½-4" from heat. Broil at 400-425°F. Do not turn fillets.

Broil steak cuts the same way, but turn fish after 4-5 minutes and broil other side for another 4-6 minutes, or until fish flakes.

Baking

Fillets will take from 15-25 minutes to bake in an oven that has been preheated to 350°F, depending on their thickness. Steak cuts will take from 25-

45 minutes, depending on the recipe. Whole fish, like flounder, trout, red snapper, or any other kosher fish, are also suitable for baking. The thicker steaks or whole fish, even the thicker fillets, should be turned over halfway through the baking time and basted after turning.

Baked Carp for Two

1 Preheat oven to 350°F.

2 On a lightly greased baking sheet, spread all the chopped onions.

3 Place fish slices on top of onions. Season with salt and pepper and place onion rings on fish. Sprinkle with matzah meal, and pour oil on top.

4 Bake for ¾-1½ hours, depending on type of fish. (Regular carp takes longer than winter carp to cook.)

Check for taste. Be careful not to burn fish. When done, fish should be crisp and tasty. Serve hot.

4-6 slices of winter carp or female regular carp

1 medium onion, chopped

1 tsp. salt, or to taste

⅛ tsp. pepper

1 medium onion, cut into thin slices (rings)

¼-⅓ cup matzah meal

¼-⅓ cup vegetable oil

Baked Tilefish for Two

**2-3 tilefish steaks,
½ lb. each**

1 tsp. salt, or to taste

2 dashes pepper

¼-⅓ tsp. garlic powder
(optional)

Paprika

2 Tbs. margarine or butter

This is a great recipe for when you need to pre-pare a quick and easy meal.

1 Preheat oven to 350°F. Wash fish steaks. Dust with salt, pepper, garlic powder, and paprika.

2 Put a generous amount of margarine under each steak and dot on top. Bake for 20-25 minutes, basting and turning fish every 10 minutes.

Good with White Sauce (see recipe in Sauces). Serve on a bed of rice or potatoes, with green vegetable salad and corn on the cob or young sweet green peas, canned or frozen.

 ## Baked Fish Steaks:
Cod, Salmon, or Halibut

**1-2 slices cod, salmon,
or halibut steaks**

1/2 tsp. salt, or to taste

Pinch of pepper

2 Tbs. butter or margarine

1 small onion, sliced thin

1/2-1 cup milk
for parve, use parve creamer

**1/2 cup matzah meal
or bread crumbs**

1 Preheat oven to 400°F. Season fish with salt and pepper. Set aside.

2 Melt butter or margarine in baking dish (about 2 minutes). Put sliced onions on bottom of the warm dish.

3 Dip fish into milk that has been salted, then dip into matzah meal or bread crumbs.

4 Place fish slices on top of onions in pan. Bake for 30-40 minutes, until brown on top. Check every 10 minutes.

Good with white sauce, cauliflower, carrots, and green vegetable salad.

Baked Whiting with Tomato Sauce

1 Preheat oven to 400°F. Wash fish and put into lightly greased baking dish. Sprinkle with salt, pepper, and garlic powder.

2 Chop onion and sprinkle on top. Pour tomato sauce over all. Bake at 400°F for 15-20 minutes.

2-4 whole whiting

¾ tsp. salt, or to taste

1-2 pinches of pepper

Garlic powder, to taste

1 small onion

6-oz. can tomato sauce

Baked Trout (1)

1 Clean trout thoroughly. Preheat oven to 400°F.

2 Dust fish with salt, pepper, and garlic powder, if using.

3 Place butter or margarine in pieces all over and under fish. Bake for 20-25 minutes, until fish flakes easily with a fork.

Don't turn the trout unless it is thick. It may then need a little longer to bake.

1-2 trout

1/2-3/4 tsp. salt

Pinch of pepper

Garlic powder, to taste
(optional)

2 Tbs. butter *or* margarine

Baked Trout (2)

1 Preheat oven to 350°F. Clean trout inside and outside. Cut off heads and tails and discard.

2 Dip fish into flour, then into matzah meal. Sauté in oil for 3-4 minutes. Transfer fish to oven-proof glass baking dish.

3 Combine wine, salt and pepper. Melt margarine or butter and add to the wine and seasoning. Pour over and inside fish. Cover pan with foil, and bake for 30 minutes, or until fish flakes easily.

2 trout,
about 1½ lbs. each

3-4 Tbs. flour

½ cup matzah meal

2 Tbs. vegetable oil

½ cup dry white wine

Salt and pepper, to taste

1½-2 Tbs. margarine
or butter

Halibut Steak in Cream of Mushroom Soup (Dairy)

2 halibut steaks
(for 2 portions)

Salt and pepper, to taste

1 10½-oz. can cream of mushroom soup

Butter or margarine

Parmesan cheese

Large Idaho potatoes
(optional)

1 Preheat oven to 300°F.

2 Wash fish and dry in paper towel. Season with salt and pepper to taste and place in a glass baking dish or a small ovenproof pot big enough to hold the fish and 1 can of soup.

3 Pour entire can of cream of mushroom soup over steaks. Dot with a few pieces of butter or margarine. Top with Parmesan cheese and bake, uncovered for 45 minutes.

4 Put a few large Idaho potatoes to bake on the oven rack at the same time, one for each serving (optional).

Good with string beans and zucchini (see recipes).

Broiled Fillets of Fish

Fish fillets

Butter or margarine

Salt and pepper

Garlic powder

This recipe can be used with any fish fillets, such as flounder, red snapper, sole, salmon, or cod. Thicker fish take a minute or two longer to broil.

1 Preheat broiler. Grease baking dish with ½-¾ Tbs. butter or margarine.

2 Wash fillets and dry in paper towel. Place on baking dish and season with salt, pepper, and garlic powder to taste. Dot each fillet with a few pieces of margarine or butter.

3 Put baking dish 4-5" from broiler flame, or at the lowest setting. Broil thin fillets at 425-450°F, 3-4 minutes on one side only. Baste twice.

For thicker fillets, like salmon or cod, turn, baste, and broil another 2 minutes. Baste once more.

Good with white sauce, mashed potatoes with spinach mixture, and carrots.

Broiled Steaks of Halibut, Salmon, Cod, or Tilefish

1 All fish steaks can be broiled the same way. Move broiling rack to 4-4½" or lowest setting from the heat. Heat the broiler to 450°F.

2 Wash fish and dry on a paper towel. Season to your taste with salt, pepper and, if you like, garlic powder.

3 Melt 1 tsp. of butter or margarine in a shallow oven-proof baking dish. Place fish on melted butter or margarine, turn over and dust with paprika.

4 Broil 4-5 minutes, baste twice, turn, baste, and broil another 2-3 minutes until golden.

2 fish steaks, 8-oz. each

Salt, pepper, and garlic powder, to taste

2-3 tsp. butter or margarine

Paprika

Serve Broiled Fish Steaks hot, with lemon wedges and white sauce or hollandaise sauce. Good with mashed potatoes and broccoli mixture, sweet green peas, or carrots.

Hints & Tips

Breaded Fish Fillets

Flounder, cod, sole, or red snapper fillets

5 Tbs. flour

5 Tbs. matzah meal or bread crumbs

1-2 eggs

1-2 Tbs. water

Salt, pepper, and garlic powder, to taste

Oil for frying

1 Prepare two large plates, one with flour and one with matzah meal or bread crumbs, 5 Tbs. of each, and one deep plate or bowl, with 1-2 eggs, well beaten. (For 2-4 fillets, you only need one egg. Add 1-2 Tbs. water to egg and mix well.)

2 Wash fillets and leave them wet so that flour will stick to them.

3 Season fillets with salt, pepper, and a little garlic powder (optional), then dip each fillet first into flour (both sides), then into egg, and then into the bread crumbs. (For thicker breading, dip fillet into flour, then egg, then flour and egg again, and then into bread crumbs.)

4 Heat the oil in frying pan and fry fish over a medium to low flame for about 3-4 minutes or until brown on one side. Turn and fry other side. Put on paper towel to absorb oil. Continue until all fillets are cooked.

If you have any fish fillets left over, they make very good sandwiches for the next day's lunch.

Fishburgers

This recipe works with fresh or frozen flounder, cod or whiting fillets, and makes 10 fish patties.

1 16-oz. package of fish

1 small onion

⅓ cup matzah meal

1 egg, beaten

1-1½ tsp. salt, or to taste

⅛ tsp. pepper, or to taste

Oil for frying

1 Wash fish, dry in paper towel, and remove any bones. If chopping by hand, cut into small pieces and chop very fine, like for hamburgers. Otherwise, use the steel blade attachment of your food processor.

2 Chop onion; add to fish. Add matzah meal, egg, salt and pepper, and mix well.

3 Form mixture into large balls, 1½" in diameter, then flatten between your wet rubber gloves or wet hands, to 2¼" x ½" thick.

4 Pour oil into a 10" frying pan and heat it. Reduce flame to medium-low. Fry each patty in the oil until brown on bottom and then turn and fry other side. You can fry 3 or 4 patties at the same time. Add more oil as needed. Place patties on paper towel to absorb oil.

Serve hot with mashed potatoes, one or two vegetables, and fresh vegetable salad. Leftovers make excellent sandwiches, even cold.

Salmon Croquettes

1 15-oz. can red salmon

1 egg, beaten

1 small onion

⅓ cup matzah meal

Pepper to taste

Oil for frying

This recipe does not need added salt, since salmon is naturally salty.

1 Remove skin and bones from fish and discard them (optional). Discard most of the liquid, but leave fish moist.

2 Chop onion and combine all ingredients except oil and mix well. Chop to attain consistency of hamburger mixture.

3 Form large balls, 2¼" in diameter, and then flatten into circles, ⅜" thick. This works best when hands or rubber gloves are slightly wet.

4 Heat oil in frying pan and fry croquettes in hot oil on medium flame until brown on bottom. Turn and fry other side. Place on paper towel to absorb oil.

Good with mashed potatoes and a vegetable, like broccoli, and/or cauliflower with white sauce (see recipes).

Salmon Loaf

This recipe, like the previous one, needs no added salt.

1 Preheat oven to 350°F. Remove bones and skin from salmon and discard (optional). Drain off most of the liquid.

2 Chop onion fine and combine with all remaining ingredients. Mix well. Grease a loaf pan and put the salmon mixture in.

3 Bake for about 45 minutes, until crispy on top.

If a larger amount is required, increase salmon by adding another 7-oz. can, 1 more egg, ¼ cup of matzah meal, and the other ½ of the can of mushroom soup. Mix well, and bake in a larger pan at 350°F for 1 hour.

Good with white sauce, potatoes in any style, and frozen creamed spinach.

1 15-oz. can red salmon

1 small onion

½ cup matzah meal

1 egg, beaten

½ 10½-oz. can cream of mushroom soup

Seasonings to taste

Margarine

Salads

SALADS

Along with the growing trend toward lighter,
yet nutritionally rich meals
has come an increased awareness of the value of
fresh vegetables in one's diet.

◆　◆　◆　◆　◆　◆　◆　◆　◆

Salads are a very important part of lunch and dinner (and in Israel, breakfast) and most people today are accustomed to having a salad along with their meals.

The usual basic salad consists of lettuce, tomatoes, and cucumbers, plus whatever other vegetables you want.

The choice of vegetables that you can add is endless! You can select from a vast array of colors and flavors and textures that can make each salad different, interesting, and appealing. You can cut in green, red, and yellow peppers, radishes, carrots, red cabbage, green onions or thinly sliced Bermuda or Spanish onions. You can even add olives, sliced zucchini, or green peas. For something really different, add orange sections, raisins, slivered almonds, or croutons. The possibilities are limited only by your imagination. Toss it all together, add some dressing, and your salad is ready to eat!

There are people who, for various reasons, cannot eat raw vegetables. In that case, you can take a few different vegetables that can be cooked, such as broccoli, cauliflower, carrots, string beans, and/or red or green sweet pepper, clean them thoroughly, cut them into bite-size pieces, then steam them for 10-20 minutes. Toss them together with your favorite dressing and you have a very delicious and colorful salad.

 This symbol indicates recipes that are quick and easy to prepare.

All of my recipes are for small quantities.
Increase the ingredients as needed.

How to Keep Lettuce Crisp

Crisp lettuce is the key to most salads. Remove
as many leaves as you will need from a head of
iceberg or romaine lettuce. Wash them very thoroughly, removing any wilted areas or brown spots.
Dry on a paper towel or in a salad spinner. Place
them in a plastic bag and close it tightly, or use a
plastic container with a tight-fitting cover. Leave it
in the refrigerator for a few hours or overnight.
Alternatively, you can roll the washed lettuce in
two (or more) paper towels, put them into a plastic
bag, and close the bag. Leave the bag in the vegetable drawer of the refrigerator until you need it
for your salad.

Salad Dressing

There are quite a few different brands and
types of salad dressing on the market. Look for the
ones that have the kosher symbol, since some contain ingredients that are not kosher. Also, watch
out for salad dressings containing dairy products,
as they should not be served with a meat meal.

I like Russian or Thousand Island dressing.
Italian dressing is very tasty, too. If you are out of
bottled dressing, you can combine 3 Tbs. of mayonnaise and 1 Tbs. of ketchup. Mix well, so that
the ketchup is completely absorbed in the mayonnaise, and you have *Russian dressing!*

To make *Italian dressing*, combine 5-6 Tbs.
olive or vegetable oil, ½ tsp. lemon juice, ½
minced clove of garlic *or* ¼ tsp. garlic powder, 1
Tbs. vinegar, a small slice of sweet red pepper,
chopped into fine pieces, and a pinch of salt.

Season to your taste and mix well.

Salads can be dressed before serving them. However, because everybody likes different amounts of seasoning on the salad, it is nice to allow each person to add dressing to his own portion.

Basic Salad

4-5 lettuce leaves

1 tomato

1 small cucumber

4 red radishes

1 small carrot

4-5 Tbs. canned chickpeas or sweet peas
(optional)

Salt and pepper, to taste

1 Wash, check, and shred lettuce into a bowl (see *Appendix B*).

2 Slice tomato, cucumber, and radishes. Cut tomato into smaller pieces, and grate carrot. Add all vegetables except chickpeas or sweet peas.

3 Add chickpeas or sweet peas, if using. Season to taste with salt and pepper, and toss.

Vegetable Salad

1 Wash and check all vegetables carefully (see *Appendix B*).

2 Slice and quarter tomatoes, slice cucumber, celery, and onion, and cut avocado into ½" cubes. Cut pepper into strips and halve them. Cut anchovies or flake tuna into bite-size pieces, if using.

3 Mix all vegetables well, separating onion slices into rings.

4 Season and dress as desired.

Party Salad

1 Wash all vegetables and check carefully (see *Appendix B*).

2 Cook string beans (see *Vegetables* chapter), and cut into 1" pieces. Shred lettuce, cut scallions into ½" pieces, and peel and dice cucumber. Halve olives, and remove pits.

3 Cut anchovies into small pieces. Combine all ingredients except tomatoes and hard-boiled eggs. Place in a glass bowl.

4 Cut tomatoes and eggs into quarters, and garnish the salad with alternating pieces of tomato and hard-boiled egg.

Serve salad dressing separately. *Serves 5 to 6.*

10-15 string beans

4-5 lettuce leaves

2-3 green onions (scallions)

1 medium cucumber

8-10 olives

1 oz. (½ can) anchovies

Salt and pepper to taste

2 tomatoes

2 hard-boiled eggs

Israeli Salad

1 large tomato

1 large cucumber

5 red radishes

A few lettuce leaves

Salt and pepper, to taste

Lemon juice, to taste

1 Dice tomato, cucumber, and radishes into very small pieces and mix together. Add shredded lettuce.

2 Season to taste with salt, pepper, and lemon juice.

This goes well with a very crisp fresh roll, hard-boiled eggs, and coffee — and perhaps with some herring as a side dish. A very good Israeli breakfast!

Tomato and Cucumber Salad

1 large or 3 small cucumbers

3-4 firm, medium-sized plum tomatoes

1 tsp. sugar, or to taste

2 tsp. olive oil

2 tsp. wine vinegar

½ tsp. salt, or to taste

Dash pepper, or to taste

1 Cut tomatoes and cucumber into thin slices (⅛"), and then into quarters.

2 Sprinkle with sugar, olive oil, and wine vinegar. Add salt and pepper to taste. Mix well.

Refrigerate a few hours. *Serve cold.*

◆　◆　◆　◆　◆　◆　◆　◆　◆

*Salads are not limited to lettuce-based vegetable salads
used to accompany the main course of a meal.
Fruit salads make wonderful appetizers or desserts,
and pasta or bean salads can function as side dishes
and even stand alone as a main course!
Add some tuna or sliced deli and you have a meal.*

◆　◆　◆　◆　◆　◆　◆　◆　◆

Tricolor Pasta Salad

1 Cook pasta according to package directions until tender but still firm. Drain and rinse under cold water twice. Set aside.

2 Heat oil in frying pan. Add mushrooms and sauté 2-3 minutes. Cool.

3 Mix mushrooms in bowl with pasta. Chop the green olives, drain the anchovies, and cut them up into small pieces. Add to pasta mixture.

4 Add additional oil, mayonnaise, and/or vinegar if desired. Season with salt and pepper, to taste. Mix well. *Serve cold.*

4 oz. tricolor rotelle or rotini pasta

½-1 Tbs. olive oil

2 oz. button mushrooms

¼ cup pitted green olives

½ of 2-oz. can flat anchovies

3 Tbs. olive oil or mayonnaise
(optional)

1 Tbs. vinegar
(optional)

Salt and pepper to taste

Hints & Tips

Bean Salad

4 oz. dried or
⅓-½ 15-oz. can kidney beans

4 oz. dried or
⅓-½ 15-oz. can chickpeas

4 oz. dried or
⅓-½ 15-oz. can lima beans

1-2 tsp. lemon vinegar

½ tsp. sugar

1-2 Tbs. vegetable oil

Salt and pepper to taste

1 small mild onion
(optional)

½ red or green pepper
(optional)

1 Cook dried beans as above or use canned beans. Drain thoroughly.

2 Mix all beans together in a bowl. Add lemon vinegar, sugar, vegetable oil, and salt and pepper to taste.

You can also slice a small, mild onion and julienne-cut half a red or green pepper. Increase amounts of vinegar, sugar, and oil to your taste.

3 Mix well and refrigerate for 24 hours. *Serve cold.*

Stuffed-Tomato Salad

This recipe serves 4.

4 medium-size
firm tomatoes

Tuna Salad or *Egg Salad*
(*see* Lunches)

1 Wash tomatoes. Cut off the tops and set them aside. Scoop out the insides and discard them. Rinse out the tomatoes and drain on a paper towel.

2 Prepare the *tuna salad* or *egg salad*.

3 Fill the insides of the tomatoes with the salad and cover with the tops you set aside before. Then place each tomato on a bed of shredded lettuce.

Serve with other vegetables and fresh buttered rolls or toast. (Use margarine for a parve meal.)

Stuffed Red- or Green-Pepper Salad

1 Take two or more small red or green peppers (one per person). Cut off the tops and set aside. Scoop out the seeds and the inside of peppers and discard them. Rinse the peppers out and drain.

2 or more small
red or green peppers

Tuna Salad or *Egg Salad*
(*see* Lunches)

2 Prepare *tuna salad* or *egg salad*.

3 Fill peppers, cover with tops, place on a bed of shredded lettuce and serve with your favorite bread.

Fresh Fruit Salad

1 medium apple

1 medium pear

1 medium orange

1 medium banana

Sweet liqueur
(optional)

The amount of fruit used depends on the number of people you want to serve. This recipe will make 2-3 good-sized portions.

1 Peel the apple and pear. Cut into slices, and then cut each slice into 2-3 pieces. Peel and section the orange, and then cut each section into 2-3 pieces. Slice banana.

2 Mix all the fruit together and serve in glass dessert dishes.

If you have company and you want to make this a fancy dish, pour a little sweet liqueur on the fruit before you mix them.

This makes a very refreshing appetizer or dessert.

Fresh Melon Salad

3 slices of pineapple

2-3 wedges of
honeydew melon

½ cantaloupe

2 wedges of watermelon,
with seeds removed

1 small bunch of green
and/or red seedless
grapes

1-2 kiwi, sliced
(optional)

This salad is especially good in the summer. It makes 6-8 portions.

1 Either cut all the melons into bite-size pieces or use a special scoop to make balls.

2 Wash the grapes well and remove from their stems.

3 Mix pineapple and melon with grapes in a large decorative bowl. Garnish with kiwi slices.

Serve as an appetizer, dessert, or at a party.

Side Dishes

Pasta and Grains

Kugels

Stuffings

SIDE DISHES

*Side dishes are very important, as they lend
an element of interest and variety to a meal.
They can often make the difference between
a dull meal and a special treat.*

◆ ◆ ◆ ◆ ◆ ◆ ◆ ◆ ◆

Some side dishes can take a longer time to prepare, but I have a few recipes that only take 40
minutes to an hour to cook. You can also buy some
packaged products that are quite good and take
even less time to cook. All you have to do is follow
the instructions on the package. However, you
must check the ingredients on each package
before you buy it. Some contain monosodium glutamate (MSG), which some people are allergic to
and others object to for health reasons. Therefore,
it is up to you to decide which, if any, packaged
products to use.

There are some products that do not contain
MSG and are still very tasty, like Rice Pilaf Mix,
and others manufactured by Casbah™. There are
probably other manufacturers, too, that don't use
MSG. Be sure to check packages for proper *kashrus*
certification before buying.

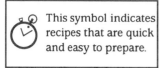
This symbol indicates
recipes that are quick
and easy to prepare.

PASTA
AND GRAINS

Pasta is known to be an Italian dish.
Some say that Marco Polo brought it back from China,
but the Italians claim that it was eaten
many centuries earlier in Italy.
Let's give them the credit; it is an Italian dish,
but it's popular the world over.

◆　　◆　　◆　　◆　　◆　　◆　　◆　　◆　　◆

For even more pasta ideas, see the Dairy and
Cheese Dishes section, beginning on page 269.

The most popular pasta is called *macaroni*. It comes in different thicknesses; the thinnest are called *angel hair* and the thickest, large tube-like noodles, are called *rigatoni*. *Spaghetti* is also very well-known — it comes in long strands.

Spaghetti can be a little difficult to eat unless you are Italian or somewhat practiced. The proper way is to hold a fork in your right hand, pick up some spaghetti with the fork, and twist it, using a large spoon held in your left hand, as support.

There are also other popular shapes such as *shells, elbows, twirls, orzo* (shaped like rice or barley), *bow ties*, and noodles that are flat and come in different widths. Bow ties are used in *"kasha varnishkes,"* elbows and shells are great for casseroles, twists for pasta salads, and flat noodles for kugels. Besides the standard golden color, pasta also comes in different colors — green spinach noodles, red tomato pasta, and brown whole-wheat pasta.

The most popular topping for spaghetti is tomato sauce, but tasty toppings can be made from various cheeses and seasonings, as well. Some people, especially children, like to sprinkle sugar and cinnamon over their pasta.

Vegetables, as well as canned tuna and salmon, can be mixed with pasta to make delicious and interesting pasta salads, casseroles, and kugels. The possibilities are limited only by your imagination!

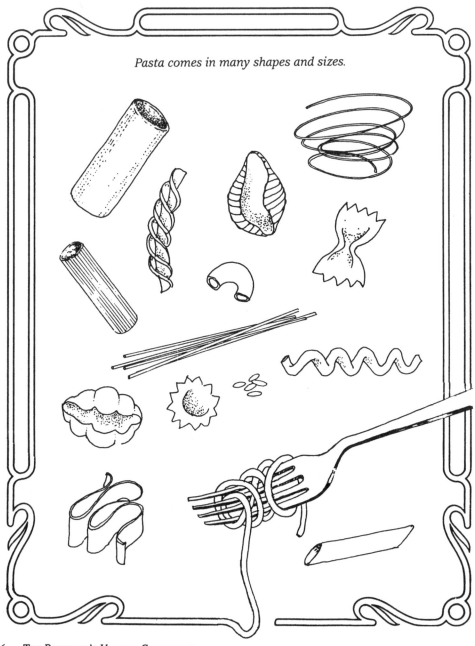

Pasta comes in many shapes and sizes.

> ### To Cook Pasta
>
> *Use a large pot and a lot of water; for 8 oz. of pasta use 3 quarts of water. Add salt to your taste (about 2 tsp.). Add pasta to rapidly boiling water and cook uncovered about 3-12 minutes depending on the thickness of the pasta. Stir every few minutes. Drain in a colander or strainer. Mix in a little oil to keep pasta from sticking together. Serve hot with your favorite sauce.*

Elbow Macaroni Casserole

1 Boil elbow macaroni as directed. Drain and add margarine or butter. Mix well. Add salt and pepper to taste.

2 Defrost the frozen vegetable. If you are using broccoli, cut it into medium to small pieces.

3 Chop the onion and sauté it together with the mushrooms in some oil. If the mushroom slices are too big, cut them in half. Add everything to macaroni and mix well.

4 Grease a casserole dish, 6" round by 3" deep. Put the macaroni mixture in and bake uncovered, at 350°F for about 15 minutes, or until slightly brown on top.

Good served with tomato sauce on top.

5 oz. small elbow macaroni

4 Tbs. margarine or butter

⅓ 10-oz. pkg. frozen broccoli florets,
or sweet green peas,
or chopped spinach

Salt, to taste

Dash of white pepper

Pinch of red pepper
(optional — it's very hot!)

1 small onion

½ 4-oz. can sliced mushrooms

Oil for sautéing

Cold Elbow Macaroni Salad

5 oz. elbow macaroni

⅓–½ 10-oz. pkg. each
of frozen broccoli
and sweet peas

1 small Spanish onion

Salt and pepper, to taste

1 small sweet red pepper

1-2 hard-boiled eggs

3-4 Tbs. mayonnaise

1 Cook elbow macaroni according to package directions. Drain and cool.

2 Cook the frozen vegetables. Chop broccoli, red pepper, and onion into small pieces, and add to macaroni.

3 Chop the hard-boiled eggs and add to macaroni mixture with peas, salt and pepper, and mayonnaise. Mix well and refrigerate.

Serve cold.

Barley Shapes with Mushrooms and Onions

8 cups water

2 tsp. salt or 1 bouillon
cube plus 1 tsp. salt

½ 8-oz. package barley
shapes

1 medium onion

½ of a 4-oz. can
of mushrooms

Oil for sautéing

2 Tbs. margarine

1 tsp. salt, or to taste

Dash of pepper

This toasted pasta product, mixed with onions and mushrooms, makes a tasty accompaniment to meat or dairy meals.

1 Fill the pot with water and add 2 tsp. salt or 1 bouillon cube and 1 tsp. salt. Bring to a rapid boil and reduce flame to medium.

2 Add barley shapes and boil about 8-10 minutes, uncovered, until soft. Drain in colander.

3 Chop the onion and slice the mushrooms. Sauté in some oil, and add barley shapes, margarine, and salt and pepper to taste.

To warm up, add a little water and stir constantly until heated through.

Rice Pilaf

This makes a very tasty side dish.

¼ cup orzo

¾ cup long-grain rice

2 cups water

1 chicken flavor
bouillon cube

4 tsp. margarine or butter

1 In a large skillet that has a lid, sauté the rice and orzo in the margarine or butter, stirring constantly until rice and orzo get dark, about 5-7 minutes.

2 Bring the water to a boil and dissolve the bouillon cube in it. Pour boiling liquid slowly over the rice, mix well, and cover the skillet.

3 Simmer on a low flame for 20-25 minutes or until all the water is absorbed. Check for taste, adding salt and pepper as needed.

Pasta and Vegetables

5 oz. of any kind of pasta
you like

½ 10-oz. package mixed
frozen vegetables

2 Tbs. olive oil

1 clove garlic

¼ tsp. salt
(optional)

½ tsp. oregano

Dash of pepper

1 Tbs. butter or margarine

A few Tbs. Parmesan
cheese, to taste

1 Partially defrost the frozen vegetables. Cook pasta according to directions on package. Drain.

2 Sauté vegetables in oil about 3 minutes. Mince garlic, add to pan, and sauté for another ½ minute.

3 Add pasta, seasonings, and butter or margarine, and stir. Sprinkle cheese on top and serve.

• Instead of Parmesan cheese, *place 3-4 slices of American cheese* on the hot pasta and let it melt. Mix through and enjoy.

• You can use *Tomato Sauce* (see *Sauces and Gravy*) for a topping. For a meat meal, instead of a cheese topping, use any meat sauce or gravy.

Rice and Mushrooms

⅓ of 16-oz. box rice

1 tsp. salt

Dash of black pepper

Dash of cayenne pepper

2-3 Tbs. margarine
or butter

1 medium onion

½ 4-oz. can mushrooms,
or 5 oz. fresh

Oil for sautéing

1 Preheat oven to 350°F.

2 Cook rice according to directions. Add salt, black and cayenne pepper, to taste (use only a little cayenne — it's very hot!). Add butter or margarine.

3 Chop onion and slice mushrooms. Sauté them in oil until golden. Stir into rice.

4 Pour into a greased casserole dish, 6" round x 3" deep, cover and bake for 10-20 minutes.

Kasha (Buckwheat Groats)

1 cup medium kasha

1 egg

1 cup water

2 Tbs. margarine

1½ tsp. salt

⅛ tsp. pepper

1 medium onion

1 4-oz. can mushrooms

Oil for sautéing

1 Heat a large frying pan without oil. Place kasha into the hot pan. Beat egg and add to kasha, stirring constantly with wooden spoon until egg is completely absorbed in the kasha.

2 Chop onion and sauté in some oil with mushrooms, cutting large pieces into halves. Add onions and mushrooms to kasha in the pan.

3 In a separate pot, boil one cup of water and add margarine, salt, and pepper. Slowly pour boiled water and seasonings into the kasha mixture.

4 Simmer, covered, for 13 minutes. Then check that kasha is soft. Let all the water simmer out, and adjust taste. Stir occasionally to fluff kasha.

Serve hot with a sauce, such as Brown Sauce, page 230. Kasha is especially delicious when served with a pot roast and topped with the gravy from the meat.

KUGELS

• • • • • • • •

Potato Kugel

This is my all-time favorite kugel! The recipe will make about 6 good portions. It can be reheated in the oven at 350°F for 20 minutes.

1 Preheat oven to 350°F.

2 Peel and grate potatoes by hand or in a food processor. Squeeze out liquid. (Some people leave liquid in — it makes the kugel moister. Either way is good.)

3 Grate onion into potatoes. Add flour, eggs, salt, and pepper. Mix well, then add 2 Tbs. of the oil.

4 Grease pan with 1 Tbs. oil. (An oven-proof glass dish, or aluminum foil pan, about 7-8" round x 1½" deep, or 8" square x 1½" deep, will hold mixture made with 6-7 potatoes.)

5 Heat the greased pan in the oven for 3-5 minutes, and then pour in mixture evenly. Bake for 1-1¼ hours, or until lightly browned on top.

6-7 large potatoes
(Idaho or white only)

1 small onion

2-3 Tbs. flour

1-2 eggs
(one is usually enough)

1½-2 tsp. salt, or to taste

Dash of pepper

2 + 1 Tbs. vegetable oil

Noodle Kugel

½ cup golden raisins

12 oz. wide noodles

4 Tbs. margarine

2 eggs

3-4 Tbs. sugar

½ tsp. cinnamon, to taste

½ tsp. salt

2 apples

This recipe is for a large kugel. To serve only 2-3, cut amounts of all ingredients in half.

1 Put raisins into a dish with water and let soak for 10-15 minutes. Drain.

2 Cook noodles according to package directions. Drain and rinse with warm water. Melt 3 Tbs. of the margarine and add to noodles.

3 Beat eggs with sugar, and add cinnamon, salt, and raisins. Add to noodles. Peel, core, and dice apples and add to noodle mixture.

4 Grease a 7½" round x 3" deep oven-proof glass baking dish with 1 Tbs. margarine and heat for 3-4 minutes. Pour noodle mixture into baking dish and bake at 375°F for ¾-1 hour.

Fast Cracker Kugel

3-4 Tbs. golden raisins

½-¾ cup orange juice

½ 12-oz. box parve, unsalted crackers

1 small apple

3-4 Tbs. sugar
(optional)

2 Tbs. + 1 tsp. margarine

1 Soak raisins in orange juice for 10-15 minutes.

2 Meanwhile, break crackers into large crumbs. Peel and dice the apple. Add orange juice, drained raisins, apple pieces, and sugar. Mix together well. Melt 2 Tbs. of margarine and add.

3 Grease small baking dish or foil pan (about 4" by 6" by 2") with 1 tsp. of margarine. Put kugel mixture into pan. Bake at 350°F for 30 minutes.

This kugel will make 3-4 portions. If you need more, proportionately increase amounts of all ingredients. *(Other dried fruits, such as apricots or prunes, may be added as well.)*

STUFFINGS
FOR TURKEY
OR CHICKEN

*A stuffed chicken or turkey is a special dish
to serve to company.*

♦　♦　♦　♦　♦　♦　♦　♦

When stuffing the bird, fill the cavity loosely, as stuffings expand during cooking. Sew up each end of the cavity with thread so that the stuffing will not fall out while cooking. The bird should be stuffed just before roasting, and any leftover cooked stuffing should be removed from the bird afterwards and refrigerated separately, so as to prevent growth of harmful bacteria.

Stuffing can also be prepared and baked in the oven in a greased casserole dish, like a kugel.

These recipes are for large amounts, since turkeys are usually prepared for holidays or Thanksgiving Day, when people invite friends and relatives. You can reduce the amount, if you want to make less for a smaller bird. For chicken, reduce the amount of each ingredient by half.

Bread Stuffing

5 cups bread pieces

2-3 stalks celery

1-2 large onions

6-8 oz. fresh, or 4-oz. canned, mushrooms

1-2 Tbs. vegetable oil

¼-½ cup margarine

Salt and pepper to taste

½-1 cup water

1 Use about ½ cup of bread for each pound of turkey. Use either white or whole-wheat, 3-day-old bread (parve). If only fresh bread is available, put slices into the oven at 250°F for about 5 minutes to dry out. Cut bread into cubes and put them into a large mixing bowl.

2 Chop celery and onions and slice mushrooms. Sauté all vegetables in oil until golden brown; mix with bread pieces. Melt margarine and add to mixture. Season to taste with salt and pepper.

3 Boil the water and add a little at a time. Don't make the stuffing too liquidy — just moist.

4 Mix all thoroughly and stuff into turkey or chicken. If baking separately, put stuffing into a well-greased baking dish. For soft stuffing, cover the dish and bake for 1 hour. For crisp stuffing, leave open. Check after 30 minutes and cover, if top is getting too crisp.

Bread Crumb Stuffing

6 oz. bread crumbs

1 medium onion

1 large potato

1-2 eggs

3-4 Tbs. margarine

¼-½ cup hot water

1 tsp. salt, or to taste

Dash of pepper, to taste

1 Preheat oven to 350°F.

2 Chop onion, mince potato, beat eggs, melt margarine, and combine all ingredients in a large mixing bowl. Check taste and adjust seasoning, if necessary. Mix well.

3 Either stuff chicken, or bake the stuffing in a pan in the oven alongside the chicken. Take out when chicken is ready or after one hour of baking, whichever is first.

Cracker Stuffing

1 Crumble crackers into small pieces and set aside. Melt margarine in boiling water. Mix with cracker crumbs.

2 Chop the onions, cut the celery stalks into small pieces, and slice mushrooms. Sauté them together in oil until golden brown.

3 Mix in eggs and add all to cracker mixture. Season to taste. (If using salted crackers, add very little salt, if any.)

4 You can either stuff the turkey or chicken, or you can put the mixture into a greased casserole dish and bake it separately. If you like it crispy, leave the cover off the casserole dish. If you like the stuffing soft, cover the dish. Bake 45 minutes to 1 hour.

1 12-oz. box parve salted-top crackers
(or unsalted, if preferred)

4 Tbs. margarine

½ cup water
or more, as needed

2 onions

2 celery stalks

1 4-oz. can mushrooms, or 6 oz. fresh mushrooms

Oil for sautéing

2 eggs

Salt and pepper, to taste

Matzah Stuffing

1 Preheat oven to 350°F.

2 Chop and sauté onion in oil until golden. Combine all ingredients in a large mixing bowl. Mix well. Mixture should be moist. If watery, add a few tablespoons of fine bread crumbs (*but not if it's Pesach!*) or a little more crumbled matzah and mix well.

3 Stuff chicken or put stuffing into lightly greased oven-proof glass or casserole dish, covered. Bake 45-60 minutes.

4-6 matzos, crumbled

1 egg, beaten

3-4 Tbs. margarine, melted

1 large onion

Oil for sautéing

½-1 4-oz. can sliced mushrooms

½ cup boiling water

1 tsp. salt, or to taste

Dash pepper, or to taste

Vegetable Stuffing

1 large onion

1-2 stalks celery

1 clove garlic

½ red pepper

1 4-oz. can mushrooms,
or ½ cup fresh
mushrooms

2-3 Tbs. vegetable oil

1 large parsnip

2 carrots

4 Tbs. matzah meal,
rolled oats,
or uncooked farina

1 egg

½-1 cup chicken broth
or 1 chicken
bouillon cube
or 1 tsp. chicken soup
mix powder dissolved in
½-1 cup hot water
(optional)

Salt and pepper, to taste

1 Preheat oven to 350°F.

2 Chop onion and celery, mince garlic, julienne-cut red pepper into ½-¾" pieces, slice fresh mushrooms, cut up parsnip, and grate carrots.

3 In a large frying pan, sauté onion, celery, garlic, red pepper, and mushrooms in oil for 5 minutes, until golden brown. Add parsnip and carrots; sauté a few minutes more.

4 Add all remaining ingredients, mix well, and season to taste.

5 Stuff bird, or put mixture into a greased casserole dish or pot. Bake for 45-60 minutes.

Sauces
and
Gravies

S A U C E S
A N D
G R A V I E S

Sauces and gravies add flavor,
moisture, and texture to food.
Gravies are usually made with the liquid
from the dish that they are to accompany,
such as meat or chicken.
Sauces use other ingredients, such as melted butter
or margarine, flour, milk, and cheese,
and are served over a variety of foods.

◆　◆　◆　◆　◆　◆　◆　◆　◆

Gravy from Chicken or Meat

The simplest way to make gravy from roast chicken or meat is to add extra water to the pan (about 2 cups) while it is cooking. When the meat is ready, so is this gravy. However, served as is, it is not very healthy, since it's over one-third fat! *Here's another way:*

Pour off the pan juices from the cooked chicken or meat. If you have a fat separator (see below), use it and discard the fat. If not, skim off as much as you can. Use only the lean (brown color) juices.

Measure pan juices and add water, if necessary, to make at least 1½ cups. Pour liquid into a small pot and heat. In a glass dish or measuring cup, combine 1-1½ Tbs. flour or cornstarch and ½ cup cold water. Mix very well to remove any lumps. Add mixture slowly to simmering pan juices and, if needed for extra flavor, stir in ½-1 tsp. soy sauce, a little at a time, testing for taste. Stir constantly while simmering, until thick enough, while contin-

This symbol indicates recipes that are quick and easy to prepare.

uing to test and adjust taste.

To make gravy more interesting, you can separately sauté mushrooms and onions and add them to the chicken or meat gravy.

After being stored in the refrigerator, leftover gravy will be very thick. To reuse: heat gravy, stirring constantly. Add very little water, 1-3 Tbs., if needed, one Tbs. at a time.

Using a Fat Separator (Gravy Skimmer™)

A fat separator is a special, small plastic cup made of dark, clear plastic that you can see through. It has a long pouring spout that starts at the bottom of the cup. Pour the pan juices into the cup, then pour them out again, slowly, into another cup or glass. What comes out first, the brown liquid, is the real meat juice or gravy. The fat has a yellow-gold color. When you reach this, stop pouring and discard the rest of the contents of the cup. You can buy this useful gadget at better housewares stores.

Hints & Tips

White Sauce

3-4 Tbs. margarine
or butter

1-2 Tbs. flour or corn-
starch

¾ cup non-dairy creamer
(or 1 cup milk
for a dairy dish)

Salt and pepper, to taste
(or ½-1 tsp. parve
chicken broth powder)

Especially good over fish and vegetables.

1 In a small pot, melt margarine or butter. Reduce flame to low and stir in flour or cornstarch.

2 Gradually add liquid and seasonings, and stir constantly for about two minutes, until desired thickness is achieved.

Serve hot. Store covered in refrigerator.

When reheating, just add a few teaspoons of water, bring to a boil over low flame, stirring constantly. If too thin, add a little flour mixed with cold water or a little cornstarch. If too thick, add more liquid.

Brown Sauce

2-3 Tbs. margarine

1-2 Tbs. flour
or cornstarch

¾ cup non-dairy creamer,
mixed with ¼ cup water

½ clove garlic
(optional)

Salt and pepper to taste
(or 1 tsp. parve chicken
broth powder)

½-1 tsp. soy sauce,
or to taste

Although this recipe contains no meat ingredients, this sauce goes well with meat dishes.

1 Melt margarine. Reduce flame, gradually add flour or cornstarch, liquids, minced garlic, if using, and seasonings. Stir constantly for about 2-3 minutes, until desired thickness is achieved.

2 Add soy sauce to give a brown color. Check seasoning. Since soy sauce is quite salty, you will find that additional salt is not needed.

Mushroom Sauce #1

For meat dishes.

1 Prepare *Brown Sauce* (see previous page). Set aside.

2 Chop the onion and sauté in oil with drained sliced mushrooms.

3 Add onions and mushrooms to brown sauce, and simmer for a few minutes.

Serve hot.

Brown Sauce

½ small onion

¼ 4-oz. can sliced mushrooms

Oil for sautéing

Mushroom Sauce #2

For dairy dishes.

1 Prepare *White Sauce* (see previous page). Set aside.

2 Chop the onion and sauté in oil with drained sliced mushrooms.

3 Add onions and mushrooms to white sauce, and simmer for a few minutes.

Serve hot.

White Sauce

½ small onion

¼ 4-oz. can sliced mushrooms

Oil for sautéing

Sweet and Sour Sauce

1 small-medium onion

½ 4-oz. can
sliced mushrooms

Oil for sautéing

1½-2 cups water

½ tsp. salt, or to taste

Pepper, to taste
a dash or 2

1½-2 tsp. sugar,
or to taste

Small pinch sour salt
or 2-3 tsp. lemon juice

1-2 Tbs. cornstarch or
flour

½ tsp. soy sauce

1 Chop onion and sauté with mushrooms in oil until golden. *(Do not burn, since burned onions give a bitter taste.)*

2 In a small pot, boil water and add onions, mushrooms, salt, pepper, and sugar. Then add lemon juice or sour salt, a very little bit at a time, until you like the taste. If too salty, add more sugar; if too sweet, add more sour salt or lemon juice. Always use very small amounts, and keep adjusting the taste until YOU are satisfied.

3 Add cornstarch or flour, ½ tsp. at a time, simmering on a very small flame and stirring constantly, until sauce reaches the thickness desired.

4 Now add the soy sauce, ¼ tsp. at a time. Mix until you have the color you want. Check taste.

Tomato Sauce

1 small onion

1 clove garlic

1½ Tbs. vegetable oil

1 16-oz. can tomatoes,
or 3-4 fresh, ripe tomatoes

½ tsp. salt, or to taste

2 dashes pepper

¼ tsp. oregano

1 bay leaf

1 Chop the onion and mince the garlic. Sauté together in oil until golden.

2 Peel and chop tomatoes. Add salt, pepper, oregano, bay leaf, and tomatoes to pan with onion and garlic. (You may have to add ½ cup of water, if using fresh tomatoes.)

3 Simmer 20 minutes, stirring until smooth. Discard bay leaf.

4 Put mixture into blender for 3-5 seconds. Adjust seasonings to taste.

Quick Tomato Sauce

1 Mince garlic (if using), chop onion, and put all ingredients into a small pot. Bring to a boil, and then reduce flame to very low.

2 Simmer for 10 minutes, stirring frequently. Adjust to your taste.

1 8-oz. can tomato sauce

¼ can water
Use tomato sauce can to measure

½ small onion

Salt and pepper, to taste

1 clove garlic
(optional)

Cheese Sauce

1 Melt butter. Stir in flour and seasonings. Mix well.

2 Add milk slowly and simmer over a low flame, stirring constantly until thickened. Add cheese and continue to stir until it's melted.

If sauce is too thick, add a few Tbs. water and mix well.

2 Tbs. butter

2 Tbs. flour

¼ tsp. salt

⅛ tsp. pepper

1 cup milk

½ cup American cheese, grated

Desserts

ASSORTED DESSERTS

Because dessert is the last part of the meal,
it is often the dish remembered most.
This is especially so when it's something
out of the ordinary, something special,
designed to satisfy that sweet tooth craving
which most people have.

◆　◆　◆　◆　◆　◆　◆　◆　◆

For everyday desserts, you can serve some fresh or canned fruit, some kosher gelatin or chocolate pudding, or a piece of cake from the bakery, with tea or coffee. However, when it comes to Shabbos, holidays, or special occasions, you might want to make something different, impressive — special.

In this book, you will find a number of desserts that take only a short time to prepare. There are some that take a little longer, but, when you see your guests' favorable reaction, you will admit that it was worth the effort.

Whipped Cream

To make a dessert taste a little out of the ordinary, dress it up with some *whipped cream*. A simple chocolate pudding topped with a little whipped cream becomes a fancy dessert. Whipped cream does even more for a piece of pie, a slice of cake, or the *strawberry soufflé* and other desserts in this book. After meat (*fleishig*) meals, use a parve whipping cream that looks and tastes like real whipped cream and is prepared the same way. For a dairy meal, you can either use the parve product or you can whip up heavy sweet cream — it's your choice. To serve, either dollop some onto each portion, or set out on the table in a pretty glass dish for everybody to help themselves.

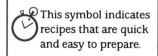 This symbol indicates recipes that are quick and easy to prepare.

Parve Whipped Cream

There are several brands of kosher non-dairy topping on the market. They usually come in 10-ounce containers that are either refrigerated or frozen. Pour the defrosted contents into a large mixing bowl and, with an electric mixer, beat at high speed for about 5 minutes or until soft peaks form. If you like it sweeter, gradually add sugar or sweetener to your taste. Store the whipped cream in a covered container in the refrigerator. It should last 2 weeks or more.

Dairy Whipped Cream

Using regular heavy sweet cream, follow the above instructions for *Parve Whipped Cream*. To sweeten dairy cream, add ½ tsp. vanilla extract and 1-3 tsp. sugar, or to your taste. Dairy whipped cream should also be stored in a covered container in the refrigerator, but it will last only a few days, since milk products sour after a short time.

Chocolate Pudding

Most brands of pudding mix call for adding milk, rendering the pudding dairy. You can also find kosher, parve pudding mixes that can be prepared with non-dairy, parve creamer, so that they can be served after a meat meal.

1 box of chocolate pudding mix

**2 cups milk
or non-dairy creamer**

A box of pudding mix makes 4 servings of half a cup.

1 Empty mix into a medium-size pot. Add milk or creamer. Stir constantly while bringing pudding to a slow boil. Remove immediately from the flame and pour into serving dishes.

2 Let cool, cover with foil or plastic wrap, and put into refrigerator overnight.

In addition to pudding mixes that require cooking, there are also instant pudding mixes available. Follow instructions on the package.

Serve with a few Tbs. of parve or dairy whipped cream.

 ## Kosher Gelatin (Jello)

1 box flavored kosher gelatin mix

2 cups water

1 Bring water to a boil in a small pot. Remove from flame, and add contents of gelatin box. Stir with a fork until powder is dissolved, about 1 minute.

2 Pour into serving dishes or a mold, and cool. Refrigerate 3 hours or longer, until jelled.

Good with whipped cream.

Homemade Applesauce

1 Peel and core the apples and cut them into chunks.

2 Simmer apples in water for about 10 minutes. Add sugar, cinnamon, and lemon juice.

3 Continue to simmer until desired consistency is reached. Adjust taste.

• For chunky applesauce, cut apples into larger pieces and cook for less time.

• For smoother applesauce, sweeten to your taste and then put into blender for 5-10 seconds or until desired consistency is reached.

5-6 apples
McIntosh, Rome, or Cortland

Water to about ¼ depth of apples

Sugar, to taste

Cinnamon, to taste

Lemon juice, to taste

 ## Baked Apples

1 Preheat oven to 350-375°F.

2 Wash apples. Using an apple corer, core them partway, leaving ¼" of the bottom, so that honey will not run out. With a fork, pierce apples in a few places all around (this keeps apples from bursting).

3 Pour a few tsp. honey into the hole of each apple and let a little run over the sides. Dust with cinnamon. (Or, mix honey, cinnamon, and 1 Tbs. melted butter or margarine, and pour into holes.)

4 Boil the water and mix with brown sugar. Pour into a glass or metal dish, and place the apples on the brown sugar-water mixture. Bake for about 30 minutes, basting a few times.

4 apples
Rome, Cortland, or Granny Smith

¼ cup honey

¾ tsp. cinnamon

1 Tbs. butter or margarine
(optional)

About ½ cup water

1-1½ Tbs. brown sugar

Fresh Fruit Cocktail with Liqueur

1 apple

1 pear

1 orange

1 banana

1 small bunch seedless
grapes (red and/or green)

4-6 Tbs. sweet liqueur,
or to taste

1-2 oz. lemon juice
(optional)

1-2 kiwis, peeled
and sliced, to garnish
(optional)

This takes only about 15 minutes to prepare and is very successful and tasty.

1 Peel and core apple and pear. Peel and section orange and remove seeds. Cut apple, pear, and orange into slices, then into thirds and put into large glass mixing bowl.

2 Peel and slice banana into ¼" slices. Remove grapes from stem, wash, and dry on paper towel. Mix well with other fruits.

3 Pour liqueur over all, and mix again. Decorate each serving with a few slices of kiwi for a dramatic effect. During the summer fruit season, add peaches, plums, and strawberries.

Bananas, apples, and pears tend to discolor quickly. You can squeeze a little lemon juice on the fruit to keep them from discoloring, but it may not go with the taste of the mixture. Therefore, it may be advisable to hold off slicing these three fruits until just before serving, then adding them to already prepared oranges and grapes. Add liqueur last.

Fresh Summer Fruit Cocktail

2 slices cantaloupe

2 slices honeydew melon

2 slices pineapple

10-15 strawberries

1 small bunch of green
or red seedless grapes

This dish can also be served as an appetizer.

1 Cut melons and pineapple into chunks. Wash strawberries, remove leaves, and cut large strawberries in half. Mix all in a bowl.

2 Wash grapes and remove from stem. Add to bowl and mix. *Serve in dessert glasses.*

Strawberry Soufflé

Your guests will never guess how easy it was to prepare this impressive dessert.

1 In a mixing bowl, beat egg white until soft peaks form. Set aside.

2 Clean strawberries, and cut them into small pieces. Put into a large, deep, mixing bowl. Either blend with an electric blender at medium speed for 5 to 10 seconds, or just use a potato masher and mash strawberries until watery, but still thick. (An electric mixer does not work well for this.)

3 Add vanilla extract and ¼ cup of sugar to strawberry mixture. Fold in ⅓ of the whipped egg whites, using a rubber spatula. Continue adding sugar and egg white in thirds until all ingredients are in the mixture.

4 Using an electric hand mixer, continue beating the mixture at medium to high speed until it increases in bulk to fill about ¾ of the mixing bowl, and becomes thick, with the consistency of sour cream. It should take about 10 minutes.

5 Pour into a shallow, oblong plastic container, about 6-7" wide, 10" long, and 2" high. Cover and put into the freezer overnight.

This very delicious dessert must be stored in the freezer, just like ice cream. To serve, spoon into fancy glass dishes and top with 2 Tbs. of whipped cream. (After a meat dinner, be sure to use parve whipped cream.)

1 egg white

1 pint fresh strawberries

1 tsp. vanilla extract

⅓ to ½ cup sugar, divided

Ten-Minute Strawberry Delight (dairy)

1 pint strawberries

4 oz. sour cream

4-5 Tbs. sugar, to taste

1 Clean strawberries and cut them into small pieces. If preparing recipe by hand, place strawberries into a wooden chopping bowl. Mash with a fork or potato masher until pulpy. Or, you can put strawberry pieces into a blender for 5 seconds, and then pour them into a deep dish.

2 Add sugar and sour cream to strawberries and mix very well, until color is a smooth, light pink.

If you want it sweeter, add sugar gradually, tasting mixture until it is to your liking.

Serve chilled.

CAKES
AND
FROSTINGS

◆ ◆ ◆ ◆ ◆ ◆ ◆ ◆ ◆

Sifting Flour

Remember to sift the flour according to the instructions in Appendix B, "Insects in Food." Since cake measurements are based on unsifted flour, measure as you pour into the sifter.

Hints & Tips

Chocolate Layer Cake

For the beginning cook, it may be best to use one of the well-known cake mixes, and then frost the cake with one of my chocolate frostings.

To make a layer cake, see *How to Assemble and Frost a Layer Cake*, in this chapter.

Lemon Cake

1 Preheat oven to 375°F.

2 Mix all ingredients together lightly. Beat with electric mixer for 2 minutes at medium speed.

3 Grease and flour 9" tube pan. Pour batter in and bake 35-40 minutes.

For a smaller cake, use half the ingredients and an 8" tube pan.

1 box Duncan Hines Supreme® cake mix

1 box lemon jello

⅓ cup oil

⅔ cup water

Grated rind of ½ a lemon

4 eggs

White Layer Cake

2 cups flour

2 tsp. baking powder

¼ tsp. salt

6 Tbs. butter or margarine

¾ cup sugar

2 eggs

¾ cup milk
or parve coffee creamer

1 tsp. vanilla

1 Preheat oven to 350°F.

2 Sift flour once. Add baking powder and salt. Sift together 3 more times.

3 Cream butter or margarine thoroughly. Add sugar gradually and mix well. Add eggs and beat very well. Add flour mixture, alternately with milk or substitute, a little at a time, beating after each addition with an electric mixer, until smooth. Add vanilla and mix.

4 Grease two 8" round baking pans or use non-stick pans, pour batter in, and bake for 40 minutes or until toothpick inserted into cake comes out clean.

Cool completely before assembling and frosting as desired. See *Frostings* and *How to Assemble a Layer Cake*, in this chapter.

White Cake with Raspberry Filling

After cakes are cooled, assemble as instructed, spreading a thick layer of raspberry (or any other flavor) preserves or marmalade, up to ½" from the edge. Then place flat side of second cake on preserves.

Sprinkle powdered sugar on top of cake. Set cake aside for 1 hour or more, before slicing.

Chocolate Layer Cake

1 Preheat oven to 350°F.

2 Grease and flour two 8" round baking pans. Set aside.

3 Mix flour, sugar, cocoa, baking soda, baking powder, and salt. Beat slowly with electric mixer for 2 minutes. Add eggs, milk or substitute, oil, and vanilla, and beat for 2 more minutes. Boil the water and stir it in. *Batter will be thin.*

4 Pour into the prepared baking pans. Bake for 30-35 minutes or until toothpick inserted in the center comes out clean.

Cool completely before frosting.

1¾ cups flour

1¾ cups sugar

¾ cup cocoa powder

1½ tsp. baking soda

1½ tsp. baking powder

½ tsp. salt

2 eggs

¾ cup milk
or non-dairy creamer

⅓ cup vegetable oil

2 tsp. vanilla extract

¾ cup water

Chocolate Brownies

⅓ cup butter
or margarine, softened

2 eggs

¾ cup flour

¾ cup sugar

⅛ tsp. salt

½ cup chocolate syrup

1½ tsp. vanilla extract

⅓-½ cup chopped
walnuts
*Leave about a dozen walnuts
whole to decorate brownies*

This recipe from start to finish takes 1 hour and makes 9-12 brownies. For larger amounts, increase all ingredients proportionately.

1 Preheat oven to 350°F.

2 Mix together butter or margarine and eggs and beat until very creamy. Add flour, sugar, and salt, and mix well. Add chocolate syrup, vanilla, and chopped walnuts. Mix very well.

3 Grease and lightly flour an 8" square baking pan. Pour the batter in.

4 Bake for about 30-40 minutes or until toothpick inserted in center comes out clean. Let cool.

5 Dust with powdered sugar or frost with chocolate frosting. Cut into squares and put a walnut half on each square.

To dust with powdered sugar, pour a little powdered sugar into a small sieve and shake over the brownies.

Open-Face Apple Cake

1 Preheat oven to 350°F.

2 To make batter, beat oil with 1 cup sugar. Add 2 of the eggs and beat. Then add vanilla, flour, salt, baking powder, and baking soda. Mix well.

3 Peel and core apples. Cut into quarters and then cut each quarter into 3 slices. Place into a mixing bowl. Dust with ½ cup sugar mixed with nutmeg or cinnamon, and walnuts and raisins, if using. Set aside.

4 Grease an 8" or 9" square baking pan. Spread batter evenly in the pan. (Use a spatula dipped in hot water.)

5 Lightly press apple slices onto dough in rows. Beat the remaining egg well and brush over apples. Then sprinkle a little sugar on apples. Bake for 45 minutes-1 hour.

½ cup vegetable oil

1 cup sugar

3 eggs

1 tsp. vanilla extract

1¼ cups flour

½ tsp. salt

1 tsp. baking powder

1 tsp. baking soda

⅓-½ cup raisins
(optional)

⅓-½ cup walnuts, chopped
(optional)

5 apples
Cortland, Rome, McIntosh, or Golden Delicious

½ cup sugar mixed with 1 tsp. nutmeg or cinnamon

Plum or Peach Cake

**10-12 plums
or 5-6 sweet peaches**

Water to boil

⅓ plus ⅔ cup sugar

1 cup flour

½ tsp. baking powder

2 eggs

**1 stick margarine,
softened**

1 Preheat oven to 350°F.

2 To remove the skin of the plums or peaches, boil water in a pot for 2-3 minutes. Remove from heat and plunge fruit into the boiling water. Remove immediately and fruit will be easy to peel.

3 Cut peeled fruit in half and discard pits. Place fruit in a mixing bowl with ⅓ cup sugar. For sour plums or peaches, increase amount of sugar to ½ cup or more. Mix and set aside for 15-30 minutes.

4 Meanwhile, put flour, ⅔ cup sugar, baking powder, eggs, and softened margarine into a large mixing bowl. Beat well until smooth.

5 Spread evenly in a greased spring-form baking pan. Place fruit *on top* of the batter, cut side up, and put into the oven. Bake 1 hour.

To test if ready, insert a toothpick into cake. If toothpick comes out clean, cake is ready. Let cake cool before removing from pan.

Chocolate Chip Cookies

This recipe makes about 50 cookies.

1 Preheat oven to 350-375°F.

2 Cream together margarine or butter, sugars, and vanilla, until smooth. Add egg and beat well. In another bowl, combine flour, salt, and baking soda and add to the mixture. Beat well until smooth. Then add the chocolate chips and nuts, and mix well.

3 Grease cookie sheet and drop cookie dough by teaspoonful onto it, leaving about 2" between each cookie. Bake for about 10 minutes.

½ cup margarine or butter

¼ cup white sugar

½ cup brown sugar

½ tsp. vanilla extract

1 egg

1 cup flour

½ tsp. salt

½ tsp. baking soda

1 cup semi-sweet
chocolate chips

⅓ cup chopped walnuts
(optional)

Chocolate Frosting

1 Put margarine and chocolate into a microwave-safe bowl and heat on Half Power for 3-3½ minutes, or until mixture is melted. Stir 2-3 times during melting. Or use a double boiler over hot water to melt the chocolate and margarine.

2 Add, one after the other, sugar, salt, vanilla, and milk, mixing well after each addition. If too thick, add boiling water, 1 tsp. at a time, mixing each time, until desired consistency is reached.

This should make enough frosting to cover two 8" cakes (1 double-layer cake). See pg. 253 for frosting instructions.

4 Tbs. margarine or butter

4-5 oz. unsweetened
chocolate

1¼-1½ cups
confectioners' sugar

⅛ tsp. salt

½ tsp. vanilla

3 tsp. milk
or parve creamer

1-2 Tbs. water, if needed

Rich Chocolate Frosting

3 oz. unsweetened
chocolate

2½ Tbs. hot water

1¼-1½ cups
confectioners' sugar

3 egg yolks

4 Tbs. butter or margarine

1 In a microwave oven, melt chocolate in a medium-size microwave-safe bowl by heating on Half Power for about 2 minutes until melted.

Alternatively, melt chocolate in top part of a double boiler, over hot water.

2 Add water and sugar, and blend. Add egg yolks, one at a time, beating well after each addition. Add butter or margarine 1 Tbs. at a time, beating thoroughly after each addition.

Creamy Chocolate Frosting

4 oz. unsweetened
chocolate

½ cup margarine
or butter, softened

⅓ cup parve coffee
creamer or milk

1¾-2 cups
powdered sugar

½ tsp. vanilla

1 Melt chocolate and margarine in the top of a double boiler or in microwave oven, in a microwave-safe mixing bowl. Stir until smooth.

2 Add milk or parve coffee creamer, a little at a time. Then add powdered sugar and vanilla, beating constantly until desired consistency is achieved.

Chocolate Glaze

A very good and quick recipe.

1 In a double boiler, melt margarine and chocolate chips over a very low flame.

2 Add the powdered sugar and the cocoa powder.
Dissolve the coffee in 1-1½ Tbs. of boiling
water; add to ingredients and stir constantly
until all ingredients are dissolved and mixture is
smooth.

Glaze a cake that has cooled. Then put it into
the refrigerator for 30 minutes, uncovered, until
the glaze hardens.

3 oz. parve semi-sweet
chocolate chips

2 oz. powdered sugar

1 tsp. cocoa

1 tsp. instant
coffee powder

1-1½ Tbs. water

2¾ Tbs. margarine
or butter

How to Assemble and Frost a Layer Cake

See also the chart on facing page.

1 To make a layer cake, bake two cakes in 8"x1½" round baking pans.

2 The two cakes will each end up with a flat bottom and a rounded top.

3 Turn one rounded top upside down to be the bottom of the cake.

4 Spread the frosting thickly on the flat side, leaving about ½" unfrosted at the edge.

5 Then place the second cake with the flat side on top of the frosting.

6 Spread the rest of the frosting all around both cakes, using a rubber spatula or a long, wide knife.

Let the cake dry for at least 1 hour before slicing.

Tip for Easy Spreading

Keep a tall glass of very hot water next to you as you work. Dip the knife or spatula into the water before picking up each daub of frosting to spread. This will make clean-up much easier. The frosting will also spread more smoothly and will have a gloss to it.

Hints & Tips

How to Assemble and Frost a Layer Cake

1 *Bake cake in two 8"x1½" round pans*

2 *Finished cakes will have rounded tops*

3 *Turn one cake upside down*

4 *Spread a thick layer of frosting up to ½" from edge*

5 *Place second cake on top of frosting*

6 *Frost sides and top of both cakes*

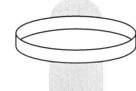

PIES

There is a saying: "Easy as pie!"
This is very misleading because
it takes practice to make a good pie dough.

◆　◆　◆　◆　◆　◆　◆　◆

I therefore recommend that the beginner buy the pie shell from the store, already prepared. You can find them in most better kosher butcher and grocery stores, in the freezer case.

All you have to do is follow instructions. If you want to bake an apple or other fruit pie, just fill it with your favorite (sliced) fruit and bake according to the directions on the package. If, during the baking, the pie begins to get too dark, put a strip of aluminum foil around the edges to keep the crust from burning.

You can also bake the shell without any filling, and fill it later with chocolate pudding or jello. For this type of pie, a cookie-crumb pie crust is good to use as well. You can make the crust yourself by using graham crackers or cookies, crushing them, and adding melted margarine or butter, or you can buy it in the store. Store-bought cookie crusts require no baking so they are great to use when you need a quick and easy dessert.

Apple Pie Filling

1 Preheat oven to 350°F. Peel and core apples, cut into slices, and put into a large mixing bowl. Sprinkle lemon juice on top and mix well to keep apples from discoloring.

2 Dust with sugar, cinnamon, and raisins (if using). Mix well and set aside.

3 With a fork, pierce pie shell in several places. Place apples in rows all over the bottom of the shell.

4 Bake for 40-50 minutes.

6 large apples
Rome, Cortland, or Granny Smith — Granny Smith will require more sugar

1-1½ tsp. lemon juice

⅓-½ cup sugar

½-¾ tsp. cinnamon or nutmeg

⅓ cup raisins
(optional)

1 8" pie shell, unbaked

Quick Chocolate Pudding Pie

1 Preheat oven to 350°F.

2 Crush cookies into very small crumbs. Melt margarine or butter, pour over cookie crumbs, and mix well.

3 Press mixture into 8" pie plate. Bake crust for 8 minutes, or until shell is ready. Remove and allow to cool.

4 Prepare chocolate pudding or pie filling according to directions on package. Pour into pie shell.

Let cool completely, and then refrigerate overnight or for a few hours, until solidified.

When serving, cut wedge, place on a serving plate, and put two or more dollops of whipped cream (see pg. 237) onto each portion.

10-12 large vanilla cookies

⅓ cup (5 Tbs. + 1 tsp.) margarine or butter

1 package (3½ oz. size) chocolate pudding or pie filling (parve or dairy)

Whipping cream for topping, parve or dairy

Easy Jello Pie

10-12 graham crackers or chocolate cookies

⅓ cup (5 Tbs. + 1 tsp.) margarine or butter

1 pkg. kosher gelatin, any flavor

Whipped cream for topping

1 Preheat oven to 350°F. Place cookies into a plastic bag and pound them with a mallet until crumbs are very small.

Alternatively, you can make crumbs in the blender, or in the food processor using the steel blade attachment.

2 Mix with melted margarine or butter and press mixture evenly into a pie dish. To make a really even pie shell, take another pie plate, the same size, and press down on the crumbs. Remove the second dish.

3 Place into oven for 8-10 minutes, or until pie shell is set and lightly browned. Remove from oven and allow to cool.

4 Prepare jello according to directions. Pour into cooled shell, and place in refrigerator for a few hours or until completely jelled (best overnight).

When serving, put two or three dollops of whipped cream on each piece of pie. See page 237 for instructions for making dairy and parve whipped cream.

Breakfast Foods

BREAKFAST
FOODS

*It is said that breakfast is
the most important meal of the day,
because the body has not had any nourishment
since the evening before.
Therefore, it is essential to eat a balanced,
wholesome meal in the morning.*

♦ ♦ ♦ ♦ ♦ ♦ ♦ ♦ ♦

It's often hard to convince people on a tight morning schedule to stop long enough to eat something. But breakfast doesn't have to take long to be healthy.

Orange juice or any other citrus drink is a good start. Or perhaps you would prefer a fresh orange or half a grapefruit. If you are in a rush, any of the healthier dry cereals need no time to prepare. There is a great variety to choose from. Just pour a cupful into a bowl, add milk, and it's ready!

A quick-cooking hot cereal like oatmeal is the next choice. This is good served with milk and perhaps a bit of sugar and cinnamon.

Besides oatmeal, there are many other kinds of hot cereal, such as Farina and Wheatena. They are readily available in stores and each carries easy-to-follow instructions for fast (often no more than 3-minute) cooking.

If you have a bit more time in the morning, an egg, either plain or in an omelet, is a good choice. Unless you are on a restricted diet forbidding or limiting eggs, this wholesome, highly nutritious food is most people's favorite breakfast dish. *(It is*

This symbol indicates recipes that are quick and easy to prepare.

certainly mine!) Eggs have been taboo in many nutritionists' eyes for many years, because of their high cholesterol content. There have, however, been some recent studies that restore eggs to the "good food" side of certain food lists. However, check with your doctor first, if you have been on a restricted, no-eggs diet.

If you are not allowed to eat eggs, you can try egg substitutes, like Egg Beaters™. (Check with your doctor.) They work well as scrambled eggs or omelets and can also be used in cooking and baking. (You can also substitute egg whites — that is, two whites for one whole egg. This works very well for kugels, pancakes, and lots of other recipes.) I have also made a number of experiments and found that some dishes that traditionally "must" have eggs in them work just as well without them. For instance, potato pancakes (*latkes*) call for one or two eggs in the mixture. I have made them without any eggs, and they came out quite tasty and very satisfactory. Similarly, meat (hamburgers) worked fine, too — just add more matzah meal or bread crumbs than the recipe calls for and add 3-4 tablespoons of cool water to make the mixture moist.

Eggs have to be handled very carefully. First, make sure you have refrigerated them carefully and see that the date on the box has not expired. If it has, the egg may still be fresh, but you should check it to be sure. This is simple to do. Fill a glass or cup with water, sufficient to float the egg. Gently drop the egg into the cup. If it floats, throw it out — there is air in the egg that may mean it is rotting inside! If the egg sinks to the bottom, it's safe to use.

Next, according to Jewish law, before using eggs for cooking, you must break each one (separately) into a glass dish. Lift the dish so you can examine the egg carefully. If it looks okay, it can be used. If it has a drop of blood in it, that egg is not kosher and should be discarded. The glass dish should be washed. *(Now you know why it's done one at a time!)*

I find that eggs taste best when they are slightly salted *after* they are cooked. If you are not allowed to have salt, use a salt substitute or another favorite spice.

It is a common practice (for kashrus reasons) to boil at least 3 eggs together, so that even if one has a blood spot, the majority do not and thus the pot remains kosher.

Hints & Tips

Hard-Boiled Eggs

1 Place eggs into a pot and fill with enough cold water to cover. Bring to a boil over high heat. Lower the flame and simmer for 10-15 minutes.

2 Remove from heat, pour out water, and immediately rinse under a steady stream of cold water.

Then either soak a few more minutes in cold water or peel immediately. The cold water makes the eggs easier to peel.

Soft-Boiled Eggs

1 Cook the same way as for *hard-boiled eggs*, but simmer only 4-5 minutes. This is a bit longer than the traditional 3-minute egg, but it is said to be safer (reducing the risk of salmonella poisoning) and the eggs will still be loose enough to taste good.

2 Remove the eggs from the boiling water and place them into egg cups or empty them into bowls.

Personally, I like to eat a soft-boiled egg with a fresh, warm onion roll.

Fried Eggs (Sunny-Side-Up)

1 Heat a frying pan. Put in a little butter or margarine. Lower the flame and slide the opened eggs into the pan slowly, to avoid breaking the yolks.

2 Fry for a few minutes, until the white solidifies and the consistency is to your taste. Remove carefully with a wide spatula, so that the yolk doesn't break. Season to taste.

How to Tell if an Egg is Hard-Boiled

To test whether an egg is hard-boiled or raw, spin the egg (still in the shell) on the table. If the egg turns very quickly (like a Chanukah dreidel), it is hard-boiled. If it does not spin smoothly but wobbles instead, then the egg is raw.

Hints & Tips

Poached Eggs

This is healthier than frying.

1 If poaching in a shallow pan, bring about 1½-2" of water to a boil; reduce heat to simmer.

2 Break each egg into a bowl (check them, of course) and slip them very carefully into the water, one at a time. Cook 3-5 minutes until whites are set and a film forms over the yolks. Remove carefully with a slotted spatula.

You can also buy an egg poacher. The pan has an insert for the raw egg to be steamed on the boiling water in the poacher. Grease poacher lightly, then simply slide an opened egg into each depression. Cook until set.

Poached eggs taste good with hot buttered toast.

 ## *Scrambled Eggs*

1 Beat one or two eggs with a fork until the white and yellow are well blended.

2 Pour the mixture into a greased, hot frying pan, over a medium flame. As edges of the egg begin to solidify and brown, move them gently with a spatula towards the center of the pan, allowing liquid to flow to the outer edges of the pan. Continue until all parts of the egg are done. Season to taste.

Omelets

The number of eggs you need depends on how many omelets you are making. Use two eggs (or ½ cup of egg substitute) for each serving.

1 Prepare the filling first. There are many different fillings you can use to make an omelet. Any already-cooked vegetables (carrots, peas, chopped broccoli) or easily cooked raw vegetables (mushrooms, onion, scallions), cut into strips or small pieces, will do. Cheeses that melt are nice, too.

2 Sauté your vegetable ingredients in hot oil in a frying pan. Put them into a bowl and set aside.

3 Pour the beaten eggs into the same hot, greased frying pan. Tilt the frying pan away from the flame so the eggs cover the bottom of the pan.

4 After a minute of frying, put all the sautéed vegetables onto the eggs. *If you wish, sprinkle pieces of your favorite cheese onto the mixture.* Fold one half of the egg base over the other half, and you're done!

My own favorite combination is mushrooms, onions, sweet red peppers, and melted cheese. I sauté the vegetables, put them on the omelet, pour the melted cheese on the vegetables, season it with salt and pepper, and fold it over.

For a meat (*fleishig*) dish, you can make an omelet without cheese but with small pieces of cold cuts. Making sure to use a *fleishig* frying pan, sauté the meat first, set aside, beat the eggs and fry them in the pan as per above. Put the pieces of meat onto the egg and fold over as usual. This makes a good, filling meal!

French Toast

2 eggs or ½ cup egg substitute

½ cup milk
(optional)

Seasonings to taste
salt, pepper, cinnamon, sugar

4 slices white bread or challah

1 Beat eggs and milk with a fork. Add seasoning.

2 Dip both sides of bread, one at a time, into egg mixture.

3 Place bread on a greased, hot frying pan. Reduce heat. When golden brown on one side, turn and fry the other side. Makes two portions.

Good with maple syrup or sugar and cinnamon.

 ## Pancakes

For a leisurely Sunday morning breakfast, pancakes can be a special treat. There are kosher pancake mixes available in the supermarket. Choose the type that you like, follow the instructions on the package, top with maple syrup or sugar and cinnamon, and enjoy!

Pancakes from Scratch

This makes 10 pancakes, 4" in diameter.

1 Sift flour again with the salt, then mix with sugar and baking powder. In another bowl, combine milk, egg, and melted butter.

2 Mix the liquid ingredients together with the dry ingredients. It's best to let this mixture chill in the refrigerator for a few hours, but it can be used this way, also.

3 Lightly grease a 10" frying pan and heat it over a medium flame. Sprinkle a few drops of cold water into the pan to test if it is hot enough. When it sizzles, pour the mixture into the pan in quarter-cupfuls. When pancakes bubble and bottoms are golden brown, turn them and fry the other side. *Use a wide spatula for easier turning*. Remove and drain on a paper towel before serving.

1 cup sifted flour

⅔ tsp. salt

2 Tbs. sugar

¼ tsp. baking powder

¾ cup milk

1 egg, beaten

2 Tbs. butter, melted

Lunch Ideas

Dairy and Cheese Dishes

Sandwiches and Light Lunches

DAIRY
AND
CHEESE DISHES

For those times that you want a dairy dish
that's tasty and easy to prepare,
try the recipes on the next few pages.
You'll find them simple, yet satisfying!

♦   ♦   ♦   ♦   ♦   ♦   ♦   ♦   ♦

Today's kosher shopper can find an impressive
selection of dairy and cheese products with kosher
certification. Not only can you choose from many
brands of cream cheese and cottage cheese of all
types, but you will also find kosher farmer cheese,
feta cheese, Gouda, provolone, Muenster, mozzarel-
la, Cheddar, Swiss cheese, Gruyere, and Parmesan,
to name a few. With the availability of all these
products, you can try out all kinds of Italian
recipes that never could be made kosher years ago.

For more pasta ideas, see Pasta and Grains, start-
ing on page 215, in addition to the recipes here.

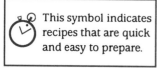
This symbol indicates
recipes that are quick
and easy to prepare.

Macaroni and Cheese

1   Preheat oven to 350°F.

2   Bring salted water to a boil, add macaroni, and cook about 8-12 minutes. Drain and rinse in colander or strainer with hot or warm water.

3   Transfer macaroni into a greased baking dish or oven-proof casserole. Dot with margarine, then sprinkle with grated cheese, and season with salt and pepper to taste.

4   Pour warm milk around edges of baking dish. Bake for 25-30 minutes. *Serve hot.*

1 cup macaroni

4 cups water with
1-1½ tsp. salt

1 Tbs. margarine

1 cup grated cheese
American yellow

Salt and pepper, to taste

⅓ cup warm milk

Macaroni and Tomato Sauce

1   Cook macaroni as directed on package. Drain and set aside.

2   Bring tomato sauce to boil. Add garlic, and simmer for 3 minutes.

3   Pour sauce over macaroni; add seasonings, if needed.

Before serving, sprinkle with Parmesan cheese (optional).

8 oz. macaroni

4 oz. canned tomato sauce

1 clove garlic, minced

Salt and pepper, to taste

Parmesan cheese, grated
(optional)

Tuna Noodle Casserole

8 oz. elbow macaroni

1 6½-oz. can solid white tuna, drained

1 10-oz. can cream of mushroom soup

Salt and pepper, to taste

¼ cup bread crumbs

2 Tbs. butter or margarine

1 Preheat oven to 350°F.

2 Cook macaroni according to package directions and drain.

3 Add tuna, mushroom soup, and seasonings to macaroni. Turn into greased casserole dish.

4 Top with bread crumbs. Dot with butter or margarine. Bake for 30 minutes.

This recipe can also be made with green peas (frozen or canned), added to above ingredients.

 ## Cauliflower Au Gratin

½ cauliflower

½ cup cheese, melted
American or other hard cheese

Clean cauliflower. Break into florets. Boil in salted water for about 15 minutes or until soft. Drain. Place on plates, and pour melted cheese over the cauliflower.

Alternatively, drain cooked cauliflower and put back in pot. Place *slices* of cheese on top of hot cauliflower, cover pot and let cheese melt. Mix through and enjoy!

String Bean Casserole

1 Preheat oven to 350°F.

2 Combine string beans, mushroom soup, and ¾ of the can of onion rings.

3 Add milk, mix gently, and place mixture into a casserole dish. Spread evenly and sprinkle the rest of the onion rings on top of string bean mixture. Bake 30 minutes.

1 16-oz. can French-cut string beans, drained

1 10-oz. can cream of mushroom soup

1 can French-fried onion rings
*by Durkee™ —
be sure it has Ⓤcertification*

¼ cup milk

Spinach Au Gratin

1 Preheat oven to 350°F. Cook spinach as directed on package and drain.

2 Rub garlic well into oven-safe glass baking dish. Fill with spinach, cover with tomato sauce or soup, and sprinkle with grated cheese. Bake until bubbly and cheese is delicately browned. *Serves 3-4.*

1 10-oz. pkg. frozen whole-leaf spinach

1 clove garlic, cut in half

1 cup tomato sauce or soup

½ cup grated Parmesan cheese

Cheese Sauce

This basic, easy-to-prepare sauce can be used on all kinds of raw or cooked vegetables. Try it on fish, such as haddock or flounder, and on noodle dishes, too, like spaghetti and elbow macaroni.

1 Melt butter. Add flour and seasoning; mix well. Stir over low heat.

2 Add milk and simmer over a very low flame, stirring occasionally, until thickened. Stir in cheese until melted.

2 Tbs. butter

2 Tbs. flour

¼ tsp. salt

⅛ tsp. pepper

1 cup milk

⅓-½ cup grated American cheese

SANDWICHES
AND
LIGHT LUNCHES

*Bread is an essential part of a meal.
The variety of rolls, breads, and bagels available
to the kosher consumer is growing all the time.
Buy from a kosher bakery or check carefully
for kosher certification when buying from a grocery
store or supermarket. Be sure to use bread products
that are parve when using them with meat meals.*

♦ ♦ ♦ ♦ ♦ ♦ ♦ ♦ ♦

There is nothing more tasty than good, fresh bread. I happen to love a nice fresh roll in the morning, but I don't like to run to the store every day. Therefore, I buy my baked goods in the morning when the store gets a fresh delivery and I buy enough to last for awhile. When I get them home, I take off what I plan to use that day and put the rest into plastic bags, close them tightly, and freeze them. When I want to use some, I take what I need from the freezer and leave it out to defrost. Bread that has been frozen when very fresh tastes almost as fresh when defrosted. You can also defrost bread products briefly in the microwave.

For hard rolls, French or Italian breads, and bagels, preheat the oven to 350°F and put them into the heated oven for three to five minutes. You'll think you just brought them from the bakery, because they will be crisp, crunchy and tasty, and the aroma in the house will be delightful! Just make sure you don't leave them in the oven too long, or they will get hard or burned.

Challah has a different consistency and cannot be heated with the same result. However, if you

have some challah left over, it makes terrific
French Toast (see *Breakfast Foods*).

Matzah: Many people buy matzah not only for
Pesach, but all year long. After Pesach, some stores
sell leftover matzah at reduced prices, but after the
matzah has sat in closed boxes on the shelf for a
few months, it often tastes stale and the crispness
is gone. Some matzah manufacturers suggest
putting it into the oven for a few minutes to freshen
it. This has never worked for me. I *have* found,
though, that if you take out five or six matzos from
a full box, put them loosely into another box, and
leave the top open, after two days, the matzah is
again crisp for a few days.

I use matzah as a good bread substitute. I eat it
with cream cheese, marmalade, or peanut butter. It
also makes a good stuffing for chickens or turkey.
See section on *Side Dishes*.

Sandwiches are a popular choice for lunch,
probably because they are so versatile. A sandwich
can be prepared in the morning and taken along
when you want to "brown-bag" it at work or
school. They're great for picnics. Sandwiches can
also be made and eaten on the spot at home —
even hot from the oven or toaster!

The selection of breads and fillings from which
you can make a sandwich is endless. Choose from
white, rye, whole wheat, and pumpernickel, "lite"
breads, French or Italian breads, bagels, and rolls
of all types, to name just a few. Spread them with
butter, margarine, mayonnaise, mustard, or ketchup.
Then top them with… anything at all! It's up to you.

Here are some ideas; use your imagination to
create a satisfying sandwich for lunch, appetizer,
or snack; to eat alone or to serve to company.

When you want a change — something for lunch that's not a sandwich and doesn't need cooking — try one of the following ideas:

Cheese Platters

On a large plate, put a few slices of American cheese, a few slices of Swiss cheese, and a hard-boiled egg.

Make a simple salad with lettuce, tomatoes, and cucumbers. Pour your favorite dressing over the salad.

Good with bread or toast. Serve with coffee, tea, or milk.

Cottage Cheese Platters

Some people, especially those on diets, may want to eliminate bread. You can mix some cottage cheese with sour cream, add some mild chopped onion or chives, mix thoroughly, and eat with a rice cake or some crackers. Lettuce and tomato and/or canned fruit can make nice additions to this platter, too.

Salads

You can also make a platter of any of the previously mentioned fish salads, served on a bed of lettuce surrounded by slices of tomato and cucumber. Enjoy along with your favorite drink.

For other ideas, see chapter on Salads, beginning on pg. 204. They all make very good lunches, with a roll or slice of bread, and coffee or your favorite drink.

Garlic Bread

1 Preheat oven to 350°F. Cut off a large section of French or Italian bread. Cut open lengthwise, spread with margarine (or butter, if using with a dairy meal).

2 Use a garlic press to mince the garlic or use minced garlic that comes in a jar. Spread the minced garlic all over the inside of the bread, top and bottom.

3 Put into oven for 5 minutes, or until crisp.

This recipe can also be made with a slice or two of any meltable cheese. Heat opened, so that cheese can melt. *Be sure you put it on a piece of foil.*

Egg Salad Sandwich

1-2 eggs

1-3 tsp. mayonnaise

¾ stalk celery, diced
(optional)

Bread or roll

Salt to taste

A few lettuce leaves

3 thin slices of tomato

1 Boil eggs for 10-15 minutes (see pg. 260). Peel and chop eggs, then mash with a fork until smooth.

2 Mix with mayonnaise. Add diced celery, if using, and mix well. Add salt to taste.

3 Spread the egg salad on a piece of bread or half a roll. Place lettuce and tomato slices on top of the egg salad. Cover with a second slice of bread or second half of roll. Cut sandwich in half.

Egg salad is especially tasty on white bread, plain or toasted. Serve with any drink, hot or cold.

Sliced Egg Sandwich

1-2 eggs

Bread

Salt, to taste

Mayonnaise

Lettuce

Tomato slices

1 Boil eggs as for *egg salad*, above, but do not chop or mash them. Instead, when they have cooled a little, slice them carefully by hand or with an egg slicer.

2 Spread some mayonnaise on each slice of bread, lay out egg slices on the bread, and top with lettuce and tomato.

Tuna Salad Sandwich

Tuna packed in water has fewer calories than that packed in oil.

1 Drain water from tuna. In a wooden chopping bowl, chop tuna with celery until very fine and smooth. Add mayonnaise and mix well. Add salt to taste, if using.

2 Spread tuna salad on your favorite bread. Place lettuce on top of tuna, then 2-3 thin slices of tomato. Cover with a second slice of bread or top of roll. Cut in half.

Refrigerate leftovers in a covered plastic container.

1 6½-oz. can tuna fish

1 stalk celery, diced

2-2½ Tbs. mayonnaise

Salt, to taste
(optional)

Lettuce

Tomato slices

Tuna Sandwich

1 Similar to *Tuna Salad*, above, but don't chop the tuna. Just spread it on your favorite buttered bread or roll.

2 Top with some lettuce and tomatoes, cover with the second slice of bread or top of roll, and cut sandwich in half.

Good with a half-sour pickle and your favorite drink.

1 6½-oz. can tuna fish

Bread

Lettuce

Tomato slices

Salmon Salad Sandwich

1 7-oz. can red salmon, drained

2-3 Tbs. mayonnaise

1 small onion

Lettuce

Bread or roll

1 Drain off most of the liquid from the salmon, but leave enough to keep salmon moist. Discard the bones and skin.

2 Chop onion.

3 Mix salmon with mayonnaise and onions. Chop the mixture together until fine.

4 Spread onto your favorite bread or roll. Add lettuce. Do not add salt, since salmon contains a lot of salt.

Drink what you like, such as milk, coffee, tea, or soda.

Salmon Sandwich

Similar to *Salmon Salad*, but don't chop salmon. Drain off most of the liquid, remove bones and skin, and spread on your favorite buttered bread.

Top with lettuce. Eat sandwich with your favorite drink.

Salmon Croquette Sandwich

See recipe in *Fish* chapter. Place 2 croquettes on buttered bread or roll, cut in half and enjoy a good lunch with your favorite drink.

Sardine Salad Sandwich

1 Chop sardines with onion and vinegar. Mix well and season to taste.

2 Spread on buttered bread or roll. Top with lettuce and tomato and second slice of bread or roll. Cut in half.

1 can sardines, with oil and bones removed

A few slices of Bermuda onion

1-2 Tbs. vinegar

1 roll or bread

Butter

Sardine Sandwich

1 Open a can of your favorite brand of sardines. Drain oil and remove bones. (Skinless and boneless sardines are also available.)

2 Spread on buttered bread, with a few lettuce leaves and two slices of tomato and/or a few thin slices of Bermuda onion. Cut on an angle and enjoy!

1 can sardines

2 slices tomato

Lettuce leaves

Butter

Bread

Super Sardine Sandwich

1 Cut roll in half and place on a plate. Spread both halves with butter or margarine. Place Swiss cheese on roll, then sardines (about 4).

2 Put slices of tomato and egg on sardines, and then put onions on top. Add a pinch of salt, if desired. Cover with second half of roll and cut in half diagonally.

Accompany this sandwich with your favorite drink.

1 fresh onion roll

Butter or margarine

¾ slice Swiss cheese

1 can imported skinless and boneless sardines

2 thin slices tomato

1 hard-boiled egg, sliced

A few mild onion rings
(Spanish or Vidalia — optional)

Pinch of salt
(optional)

Super Nova Sandwich

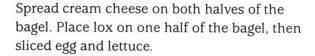

1 fresh bagel, cut open

1-1½ Tbs. cream cheese

1 oz. Nova Scotia
(unsalted) lox

½-1 hard-boiled egg,
sliced

Lettuce leaf

1-2 slices mild onion
(optional)

Spread cream cheese on both halves of the bagel. Place lox on one half of the bagel, then sliced egg and lettuce.

Top with onion, if desired. Cover with other half of bagel and cut in half.

Have it with your favorite drink.

Fish Sandwiches

Use *Fishburgers* (see pg. 199), made fresh or left over from dinner, either cold or warmed up. Spread two slices of bread or both halves of a roll with margarine, butter, or mayonnaise. Place burger on one slice of bread or half of roll, top with lettuce and tomatoes, if you like, cover, and enjoy.

Great with coffee, tea or milk, and fruit or pastry for dessert.

Other delicious sandwiches can be made from leftover fish made for dinner the night before, like flounder, sole, or salmon fillet. Just put a little mayonnaise, mustard, or butter on some bread or a roll, then the fish fillet. It may even be a good idea to intentionally prepare a little more fish than you need at dinner and leave it for the next day's lunch. You can also use some of the fish steaks that contain very few bones, such as halibut or salmon, but be sure to remove *all* of the bones before you make the sandwich.

Cheese Sandwiches

There are many different cheeses on the market suitable for sandwich making; Swiss, American, and cream cheese are just some examples.

Spread the cheese or place the slices on bread or a roll. Add some slices of hard-boiled egg, a sliced pickle, perhaps some lettuce and/or tomato, and cover with the other slice or top of roll.

Cut sandwich in half. *Try one of my favorites: thin dark pumpernickel bread with cream cheese.*

The One-Minute Grilled Cheese Sandwich

1 Place 1 or 2 slices of American cheese between 2 slices of white bread. Season cheese to taste.

2 Heat a small frying pan. Add a little butter or margarine (about ½-¾ tsp.). Place cheese sandwich in frying pan, reduce heat to very low. Put a small piece of foil on top of sandwich and press down with another small (dairy) pot for 10-15 seconds or until bread is lightly browned (do not burn). Turn and repeat.

Cut sandwich diagonally. Serve hot.

Good with cold milk, chocolate milk, or coffee.

1-2 slices American cheese

2 slices white bread

Salt to taste

Margarine or butter

For a change of pace, make a meat sandwich. Most butcher shops and many kosher grocery stores carry various types of delicatessen meats in vacuum packages or sliced to order. They are ideal for sandwiches, on rolls or whatever bread you like. Some healthy choices are sliced turkey, white or dark meat, boiled or smoked, and chicken or turkey salami slices.

Turkey or Chicken Sandwich

1 piece Italian bread, about 6-7" long
or any other kind of bread or roll you prefer

Mayonnaise

6-8 slices of cold cuts

Sour pickle

Mustard
optional

Ketchup
optional

I like to mix white boiled turkey with smoked pastrami from vacuum-sealed packages to make filling and tasty sandwiches on oven-heated parve Italian bread.

1 Heat the bread in the oven for a few minutes until crispy. Wait until the bread is cool, then cut it open.

2 Spread mayonnaise on the bread, put meat and sour pickle in place, add mustard and/or ketchup, if desired.

Put top of bread on and you are ready to enjoy a delicious sandwich with tea or coffee (whitened with parve coffee lightener) or any soda you like.

Salami or Bologna Sandwich

1 If you are serving French fries as a side dish, start these first, according to the package directions, so they will be ready when the sandwich is finished.

2 Spread mayonnaise/mustard/ketchup on bread. Cover with as many slices of meat as you wish. Top with second slice of bread. *Enjoy!*

2 slices bread

Mayonnaise, mustard and/or ketchup to taste
(optional)

Sliced salami *or* bologna

Frozen French fried potatoes as side dish
(optional)

Hamburger on a Bun

If you had *hamburger patties* or *meatloaf* (see *Ground Meat Dishes,* pg. 183) for dinner the night before, use the leftovers, warmed up or cold. Serve on a hamburger roll with ketchup and thinly sliced Spanish or Vidalia onion. Enjoy your favorite cold or hot drink alongside.

For dessert, try fresh fruit, parve cookies, or cake.

Frankfurter on a Roll

Before boiling franks, pierce them in 2-3 places with a fork, to prevent them from bursting. Put them in a pot of water and boil for about 15 minutes.

Remove from water with a fork and place on roll. Spread with mustard and/or ketchup and, if you like, some sauerkraut.

Great with tea or soda.

Frankfurters and Beans

2-3 frankfurters

1 small can vegetarian
baked beans

1-2 slices of bread or roll

1 Boil frankfurters in a pot of water for 15 minutes, as above; remove from water with a fork, and cut into ½" slices.

2 In another pot, heat the beans according to the directions on the can. Mix beans and frankfurter slices and serve on a plate with bread or roll.

You may want a parve danish with tea or fresh fruit for dessert.

Chicken or Turkey Salad Sandwich

¼ of a cooked chicken
or turkey
white and/or dark meat

1 stalk celery

1½-2 Tbs. mayonnaise

Salt and pepper, to taste

2 slices of bread or a roll

Lettuce

½ tomato, sliced thin

1 half-sour or sour pickle

Here's a great way to use up leftover chicken or turkey.

1 Remove skin and bones from chicken or turkey. Cut meat into small bite-size pieces.

2 Dice celery and combine with chopped chicken or turkey. Add as much mayonnaise as you like. Mix well and season with salt and pepper to taste.

3 Spread a small amount of mayonnaise on the bread or roll, then the chicken or turkey salad. Top with lettuce and tomato. Cover with second piece of bread or top of roll, and cut in half. Serve the pickle on the side.

Enjoy sandwich along with your favorite drink.

Appendices

Appendix A

KASHERING MEAT

◆   ◆   ◆   ◆   ◆   ◆   ◆   ◆   ◆

Meat that has been slaughtered properly and porged is still not ready for cooking until it is kashered — made kosher — by removing its blood. This is accomplished by either of two processes: salting or broiling. Until not so long ago, salting meat was one of the major activities of the Jewish homemaker. Today, it is a rarity for meat to be sold as kosher unless it has already been salted. Nevertheless, people on salt-free diets can obtain kosher meat before salting and broil it themselves. An even more relevant situation is that of liver. Liver is so saturated with blood that the salting process is incapable of rendering it blood-free. All liver must therefore be broiled before consumption. While kashered liver is commonly sold, many kosher establishments do sell liver raw — leaving the kashering to the consumer.

Salting

As the need for kashering one's own meat today is highly uncommon, a brief and general description of the salting process should suffice.

The salting process involves three stages: soaking, salting, and rinsing. The meat is first soaked in room-temperature water for half an hour, and then rinsed and drained until most — but not all — of the water has disappeared. The meat is then completely coated in coarse salt (including insides of grooves) and positioned in a way that allows for the blood to drain (e.g., on wooden slats, a tray with holes, or on any smooth slanted surface) for the duration of an hour. Finally the meat is rinsed well three times. Ideally, meat should be salted within 72 hours of slaughter. Many authorities do permit the salting of meat that was frozen soon after slaughter. In this case, it is salted just after defrosting, regardless of how long the meat remained frozen.

Broiling

Prior to broiling, meat should be rinsed to remove surface blood. In the case of liver, if it is to be broiled whole, there is a need for criss-cross slitting to allow for the blood to drain. The meat is placed on a metal grate, lightly sprinkled with salt, and immediately placed over the fire. (The meat should not be wrapped in foil.)

The meat should not be removed from the fire until the surface is dry; it is customary to continue broiling until it is slightly singed. Upon removal from the fire, the meat is to be rinsed immediately three times.

Traditionally, broiling was done over an open flame. Some authorities permit use of a broiler. It is advisable to consult a halachic authority about the details of kashering liver in the broiler of an oven.

Appendix B

INSECTS
IN FOOD

♦ ♦ ♦ ♦ ♦ ♦ ♦ ♦ ♦

All fruits and vegetables that are commonly insect-infested require inspection prior to use. The area of the fruit or vegetables where insects are often found must be carefully examined. While the amount of infestation can vary on the basis of climate and the use of insecticides, there are some general rules one should be familiar with.

Different foods are appealing to the insect for different reasons, including nourishment, shelter, and an appropriate environment for laying eggs. Awareness of just what the particular food has to offer from the insect's perspective is the key to determining which part of the food is in need of inspection.

Nourishment

A. Sugar — Most insects have a sweet-tooth! As a precautionary measure, one should keep all sweet foods well sealed to prevent infestation. Before using a bag of sugar that was left unsealed, one must check to see that the sugar is free of ants. Fruits that are especially sweet, including dates, figs, carob, and sweet cherries, must be carefully examined — inside and out — as they attract a variety of insects and maggots.

B. Protein — Grains attract worms who live off the protein content and lay eggs as well. Grain kernels must be inspected — looking out for weevils between the grains and worm-holes on the surface of the grain. Flour must be sifted through a fine sieve before baking. (Bran has no protein and is rarely infested.)

C. **Other nutriments** — Parasites often attach themselves to the arteries of leafy vegetables and live off the leaves. The various insects — especially aphids — are similar in color to the leaves and difficult to detect. Soaking the leaf in salt water or diluted vinegar and then rinsing under pressure helps get rid of many of the insects but careful inspection of individual leaves is still necessary. Lettuce, cabbage, celery leaves, parsley, dill, mint, and even strawberry leaves cannot be used without thorough inspection. (One can, however, tie dill, mint, or parsley in a special gourmet bag to add flavor to a stew, as the insects would not permeate the bag.)

Shelter

A. **Camouflage** — There is no safer haven for an insect than between the grooves of broccoli or cauliflower. Bugs are virtually undetectable whether the vegetables are fresh or frozen. Spinach, too, has numerous concealed places to hide in. These vegetables are so difficult to clean that many people avoid using them altogether. In order to use such vegetables, one can soak them in a bowl of water, agitate the water, and then look for tiny insects in the bowl and on the base and florets of the vegetable. If insects are spotted, the bowl is emptied, refilled with fresh water, and the process is repeated until the water is found to be insect-free. This method is not foolproof, but acceptable halachically. The inside of a celery stalk should be scrubbed thoroughly to insure that no insects are hiding inside. Another common situation is that of tiny insects dwelling on the peel of fruit, posing as dirt or discoloration. Therefore, for example, citrus rind cannot be grated for baking without first being scrubbed.

B. *Protection* — The skin of a bean may easily be hiding an insect. Beans must be soaked overnight to loosen the skin and render it translucent so that bugs can be spotted.

Also, corn on the cob may contain a complex system of tunnels filled with insects. The cob should be sliced so that one can investigate just what is going on beneath the surface.

Among insects, a favorite spot for raising a family is on the pit of a fruit. All summer fruit (peaches, plums, apricots) must be opened before use and the area around the pit inspected. The inside of a nut can also be infested with insects and eggs and the nut should be halved.

Additionally, old packages of dried fruit, grain products, and sweets should be examined to see that mites haven't moved in. Webbing in a package is a sign of infestation — and a sign that use of the package had better be avoided.

In conclusion, inspection for insects is a tedious but integral aspect of keeping kosher. One just does not use regularly infested foods unless he has the time to carefully examine them. It is best to use insect-free fresh and frozen vegetables with *kashrus* certification. One should approach a competent Rabbinic authority with specific questions regarding this subject.

Appendix C

KITCHEN TOOLS

◆　◆　◆　◆　◆　◆　◆　◆　◆

Every kitchen needs at least the basic cooking and baking utensils. Just like any mechanic who cannot do his job without his hammer, pliers, and screwdriver as his basic tools, so, too, a cook must have his or her basic pots and pans and knives, among many other cooking tools and gadgets that save time and work. In addition, a strictly kosher kitchen must have many items in duplicate: one for meat and one for dairy — and possibly a third for parve! (Not to mention yet a fourth and fifth and possibly sixth for Pesach!)

However, you don't have to buy all the things needed in a kitchen all at once. Buy what you need as you need it. Nor do you have to "break the bank." I have bought some very good kitchen equipment and tools in discount stores for very low prices, compared to houseware specialty stores.

All you really need to start with are a few pots of different sizes, one or two frying pans, sharp knives, a vegetable peeler, pot holders and/or oven mitts, and a baking pan. The rest you can pick up when you know what you need or you see something in a store that you would like to add to your collection.

When you buy any pots or frying pans, try to get only stainless steel. These will last a very long time, especially if they are of the heavier quality. You can sometimes get the better-known brands

on sale, either individually or in sets of a number of different sized pots and a frying pan. Avoid enamel pots, as they tend to chip easily and must be discarded if the chips are on the inside, where the food cooks. Whichever pots and pans you buy, be sure they have handles that do *not* get hot during cooking (such as wood or heavy plastic). Some pots are designed for use in the oven as well as on top of the stove. The handles of such oven-proof pots still get very hot — always use oven mitts or pot holders!

For use in the oven, you can get a few Pyrex™ (oven-proof tempered glass) pans in various sizes. These are very good for baking fish, kugels, and casseroles. A non-stick frying pan comes in very handy, is easy to clean, and you don't have to use too much oil or other fats to fry your food in it. Every kitchen should have one large, heavy pot (a Dutch oven or stock pot). It is ideal for cooking chicken or pot roast.

An electric mixer is a very handy tool to have. A simple hand mixer is inexpensive — watch for store sales. If you will do a lot of mixing, get an electric blender. It will come in handy for making sauces and blending vegetables into soups. Blenders too can often be bought on sale.

You will also need a wooden chopping bowl and a chopping knife, as well as other sharp knives and a cutting board. You will find you'll have a hundred uses for them.

You may be able to find a small slicing tool in stores selling housewares. However, it seems to have disappeared from most places, replaced by the food processor, perhaps. There are small slicers for cheese, eggs, and tomatoes, which can cut fairly even slices. I prefer to use a sharp knife for tomatoes and onions, but I do have an egg slicer and a cheese slicer. They tend to be very inexpensive, and every kitchen should have one.

A knife sharpener comes in very handy, since knives do get dull eventually. Sharp knives are very important in cutting your meats, vegetables, rolls, etc., so you must maintain them. Some electric can openers have sharpeners built in. They work quite well.

On the next two pages are some illustrations of various kitchen tools, gadgets, and pots and pans, to give you an idea of what to look for. Start out buying *only* what you need and plan to use. As you become more advanced in your cooking, you will see what you are missing and you will look to add more items to your collection.

pastry blender

rubber spatula

electric mixer

measuring spoons

Knives

baking pans

grater

cookie sheet

pots and pans

frying pans

roaster

glass mixing bowls

pot holder

strainer

mallet for tenderizing meat

potato masher

long oven mitts

measuring cups

wooden chopping bowl and chopping knife

baster

wooden spoon

spatula

liver broiler

colander

vegetable peeler

INDEX

Basic Shopping List

Try to always have on hand all of the food staples, paper goods, and cleaning supplies you ordinarily use. Buy perishables only as you need them, and use them up.

Food Staples

Flour	Rice	Mustard
Sugar	Matzah Meal	Salad Dressing
Salt	Tomato Sauce	Dried soup mix
Pepper	Tomato Paste	Dried beans
Spices	Mushroom soup	Coffee/Tea
Tuna/Salmon	Mayonnaise	Creamer
Oil/Shortening	Horseradish	Cold and hot cereals
Pasta	Ketchup	

Paper Goods and Cleaning Supplies

Garbage bags	Disposable dishes
Food storage bags	Plastic tableware
Aluminum foil	*knives/forks/spoons*
Plastic wrap	Dish detergent
Napkins	Sponges
Paper towels	Scrubbers
Plastic or paper cups	Steel wool
hot/cold	

Perishables

Meat and Poultry:	Fruit	Bread
Chicken, Turkey,	Eggs	*Challos, Rolls,*
Beef, Veal	Milk	*Bagels, Pita*
Fish	Butter	Juices
Gefilte fish *(frozen, jarred)*	Cheeses	*Grape, Orange,*
Vegetables	Cakes/Desserts	*Apple, Cranberry*